GATE-KEEPERS

URBAN HEROES

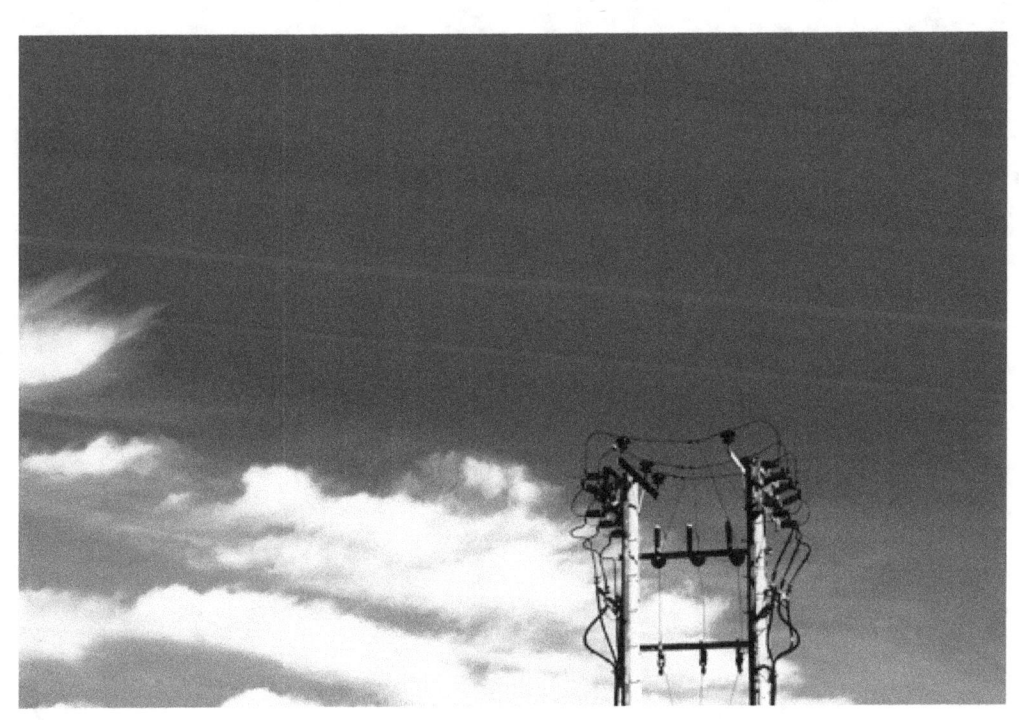

G. P. Moci

ATHENS 2019

FOR MY SILENT FRIENDS

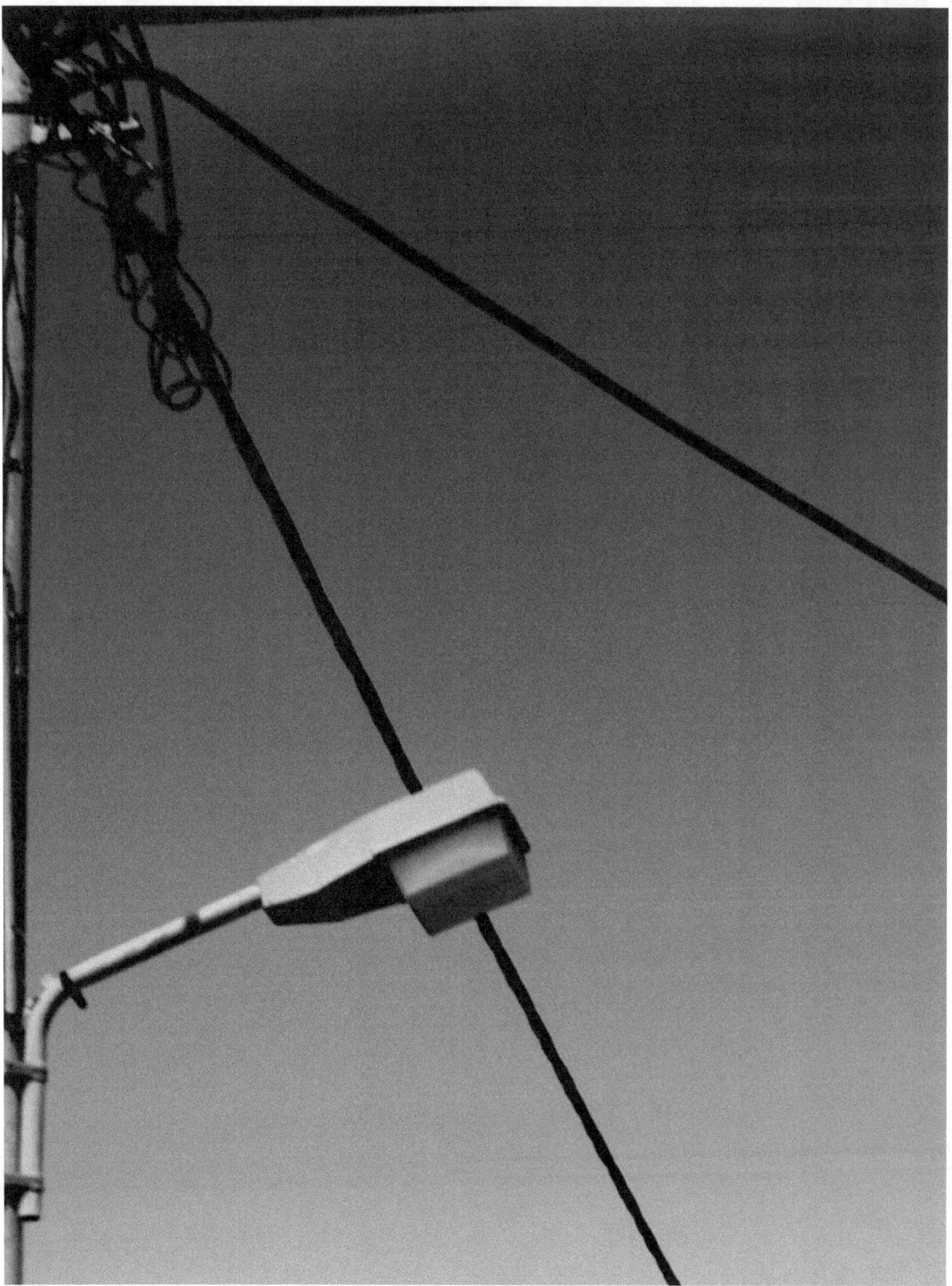

ABSTRACT

I find poetry in these photos, I capture figures, urban heroes to whom I find a heroic silence. This series of photos is not a different view of the sky. Most of the photographs of this series capture the figures that rise and stand above us as if they are guarding and framing the gates of the universe, the sky itself.

I followed the fellowship of the skyline in the city of Athens, next to the buildings trying to find the Gatekeepers on their most romantic moments. It was a game of light and shadow, trying to frame compositions which would reveal their loneliness and expose their greatness. In these photos, I have carefully chosen the characters because they carry the narration of all the lonely and proud Heroes of my city.

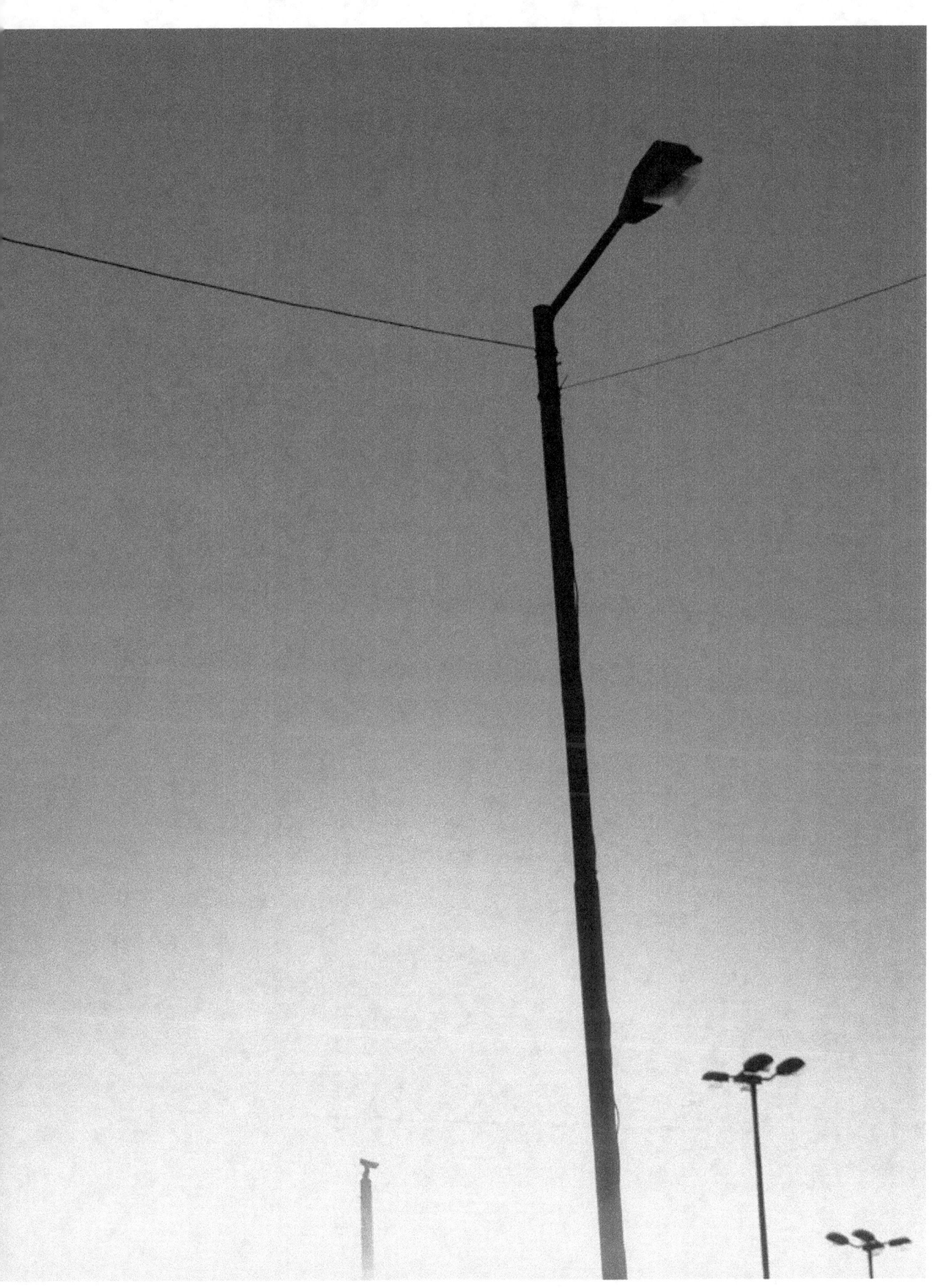

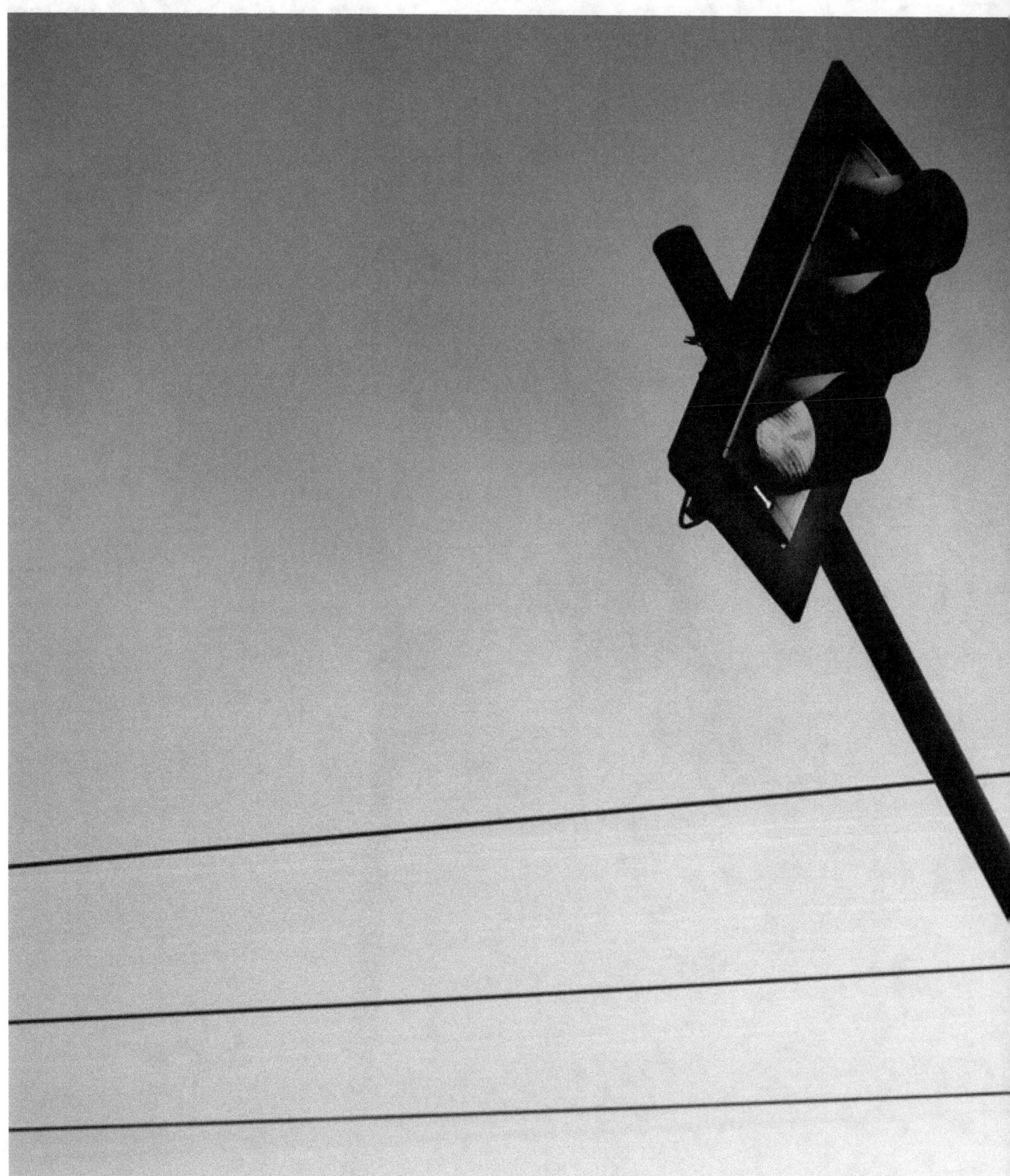

Busy
skies
&
Traffic
lines

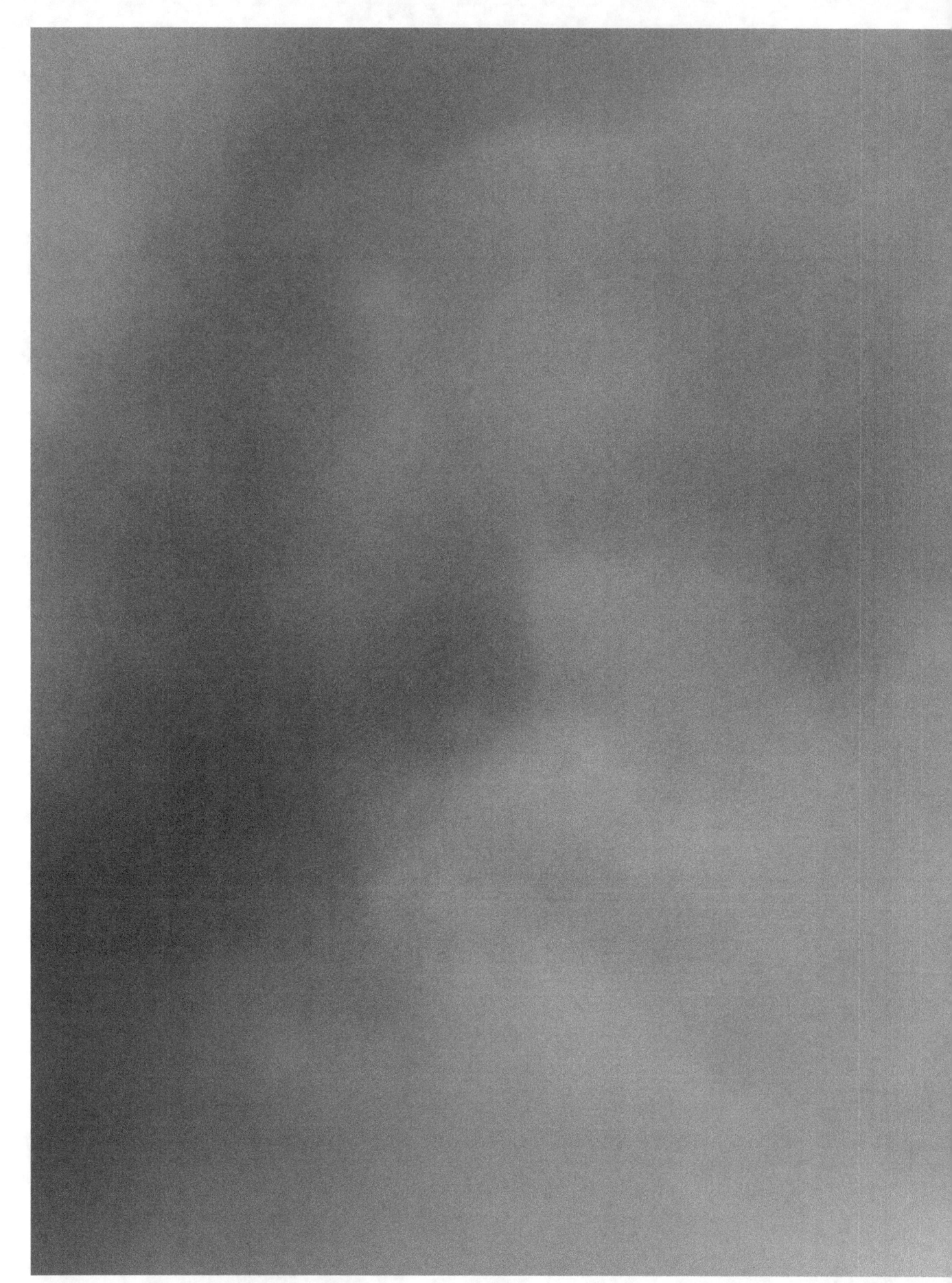

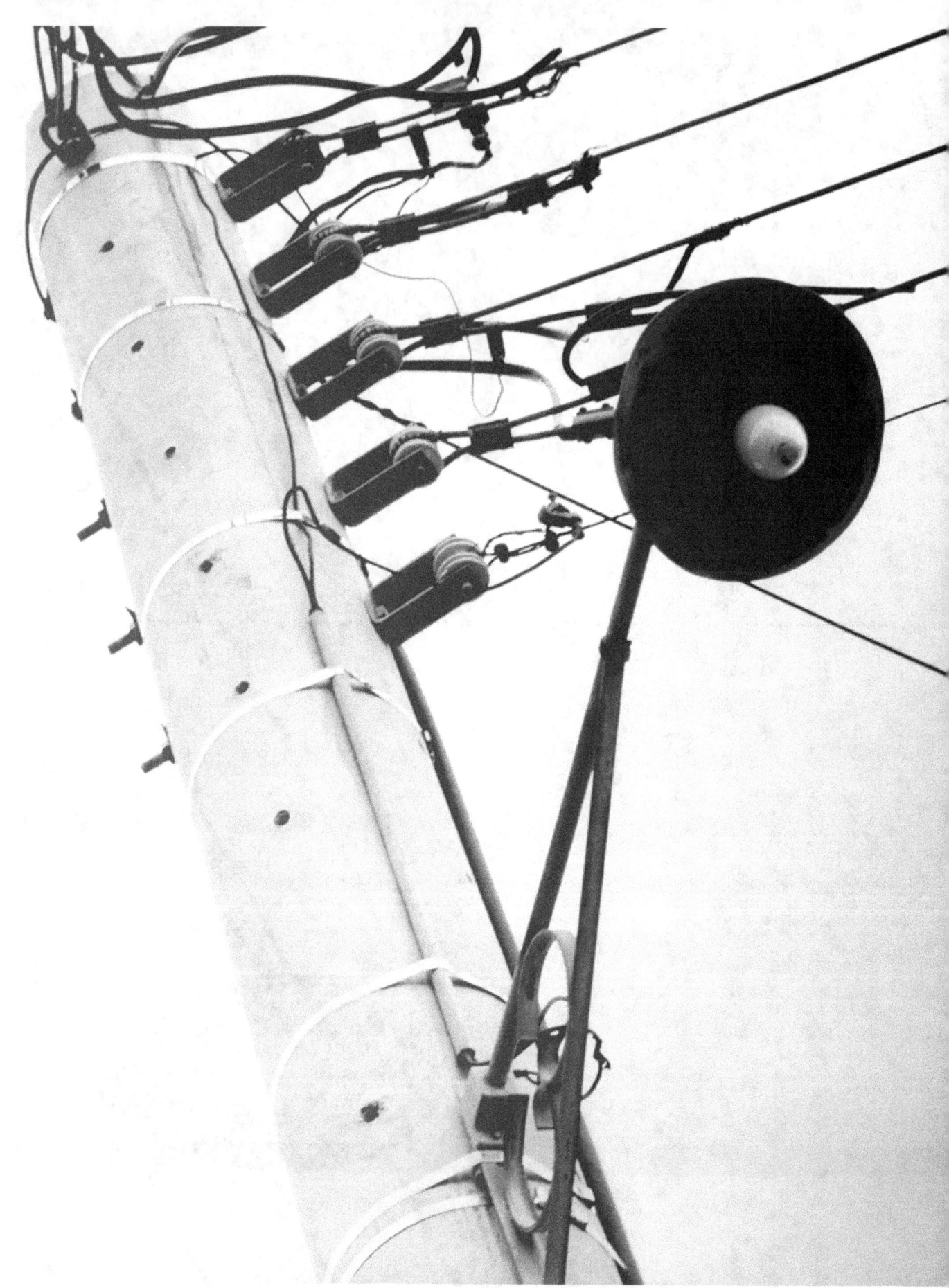

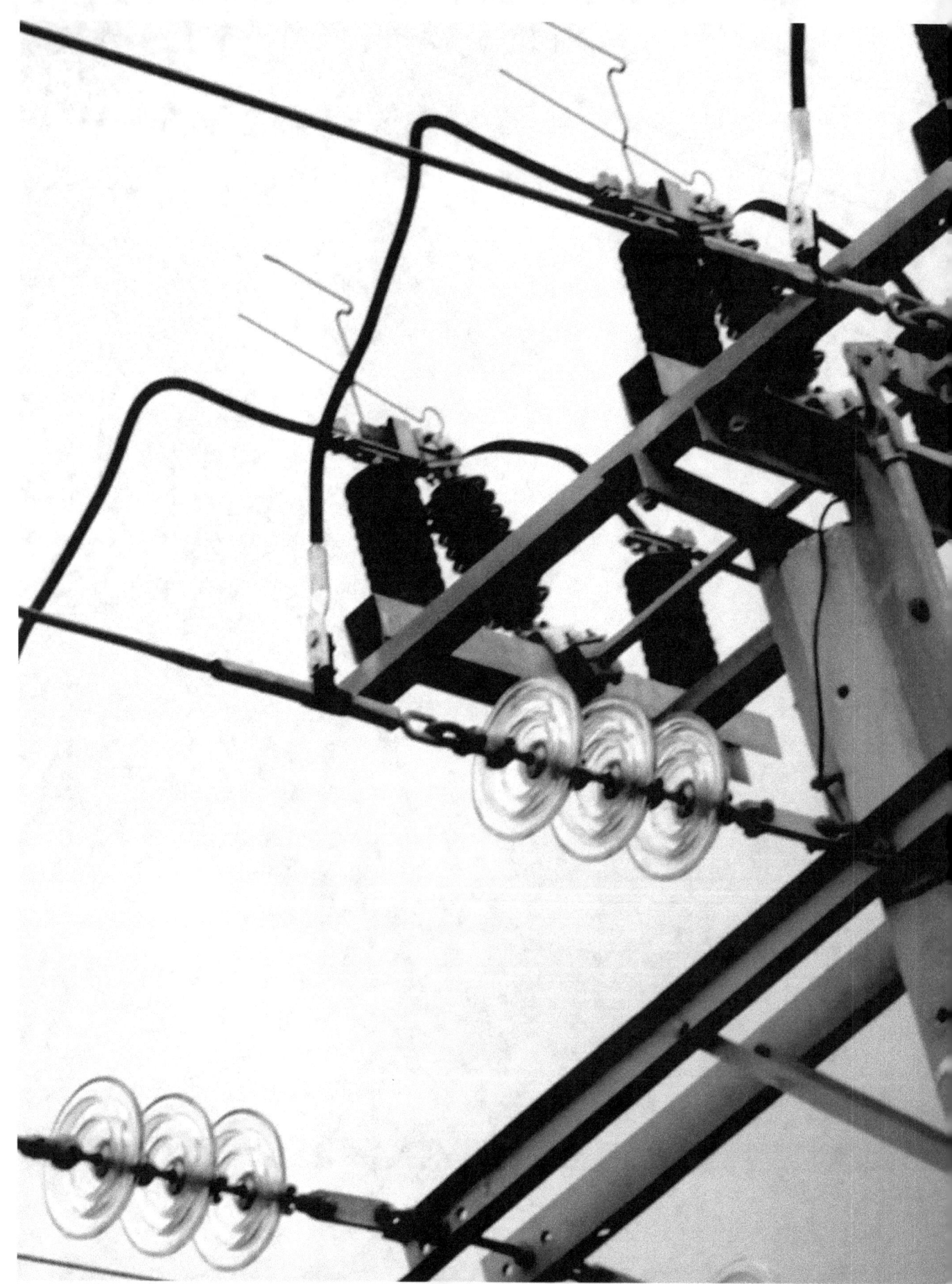

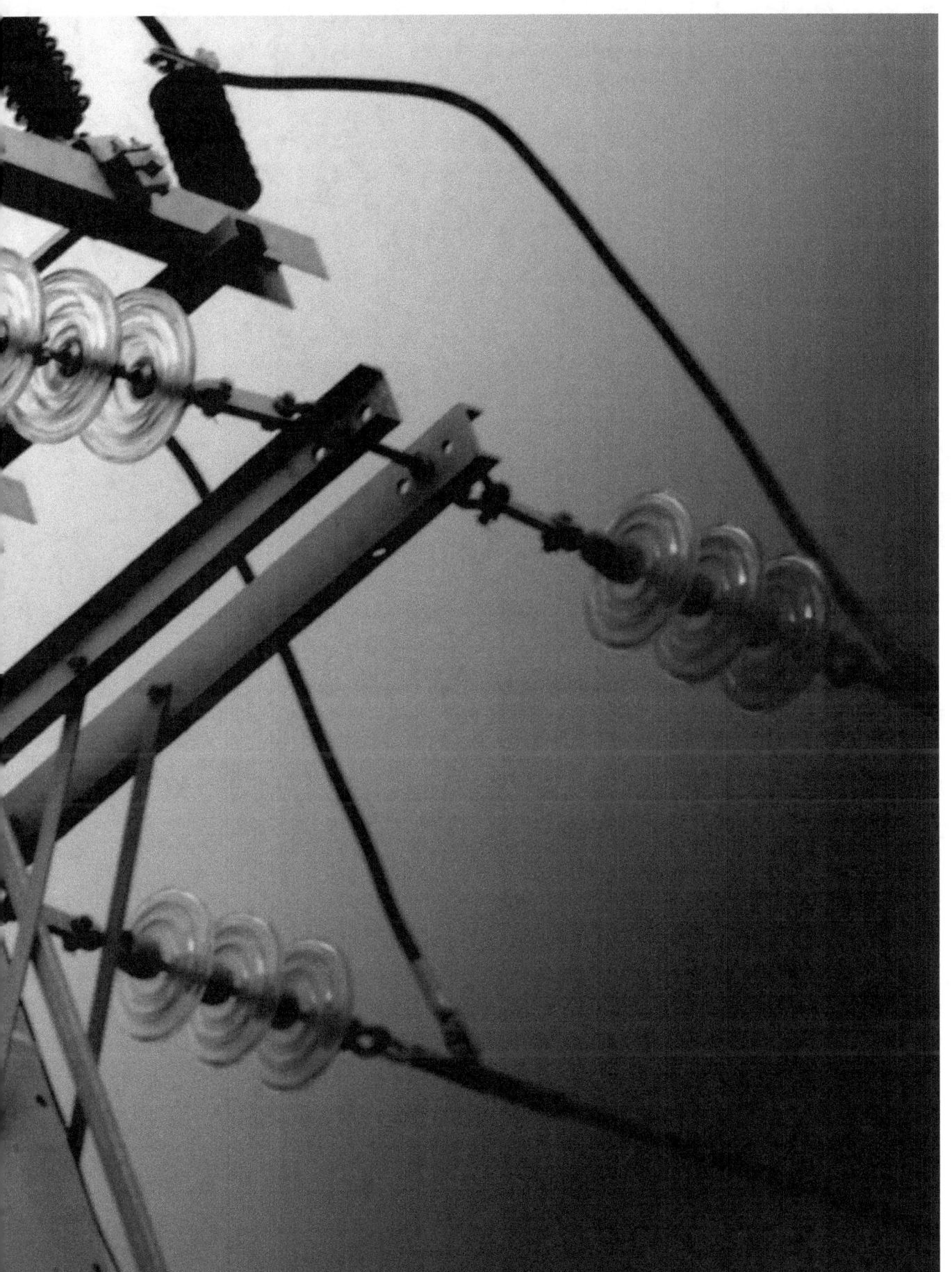

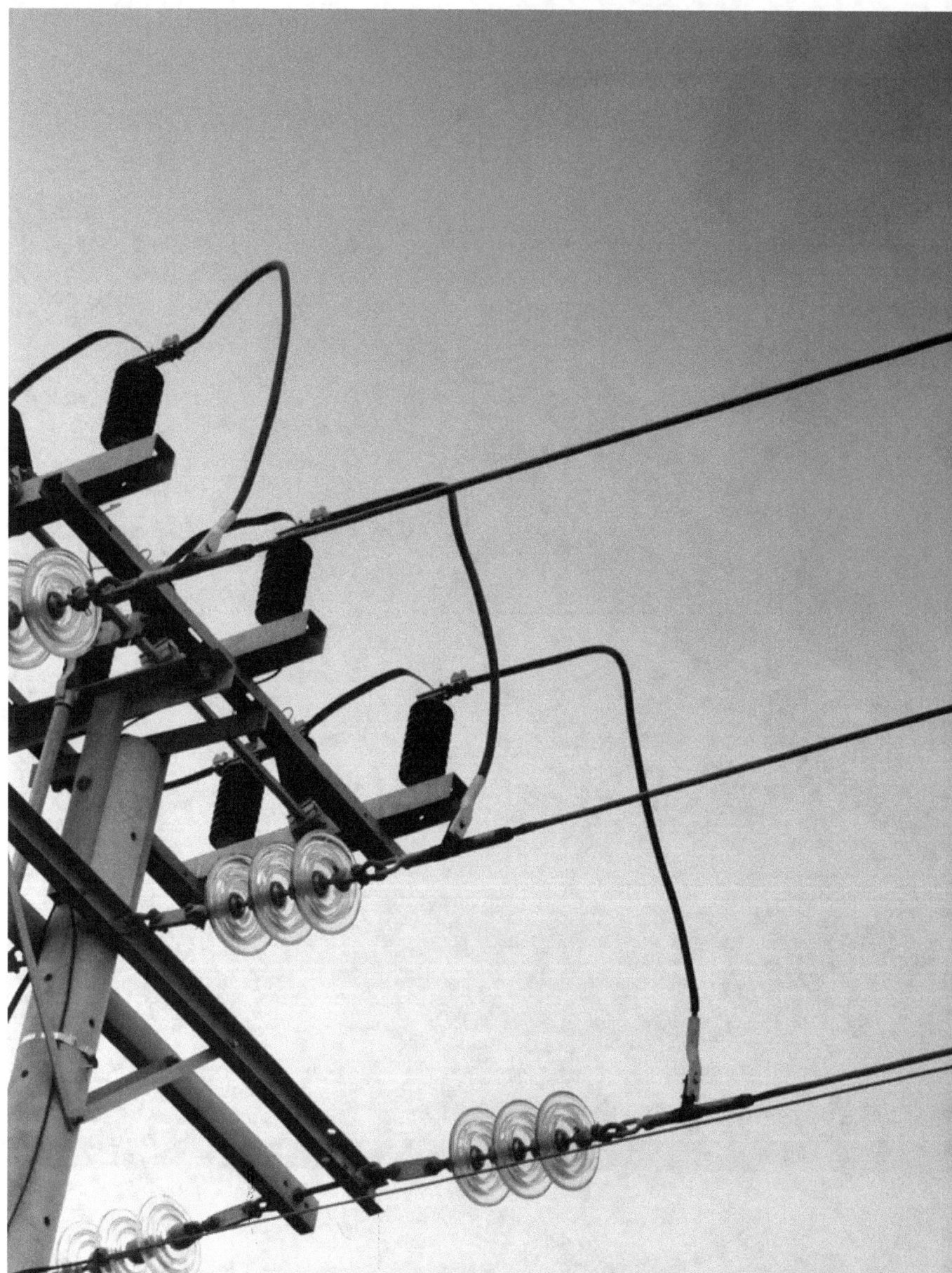

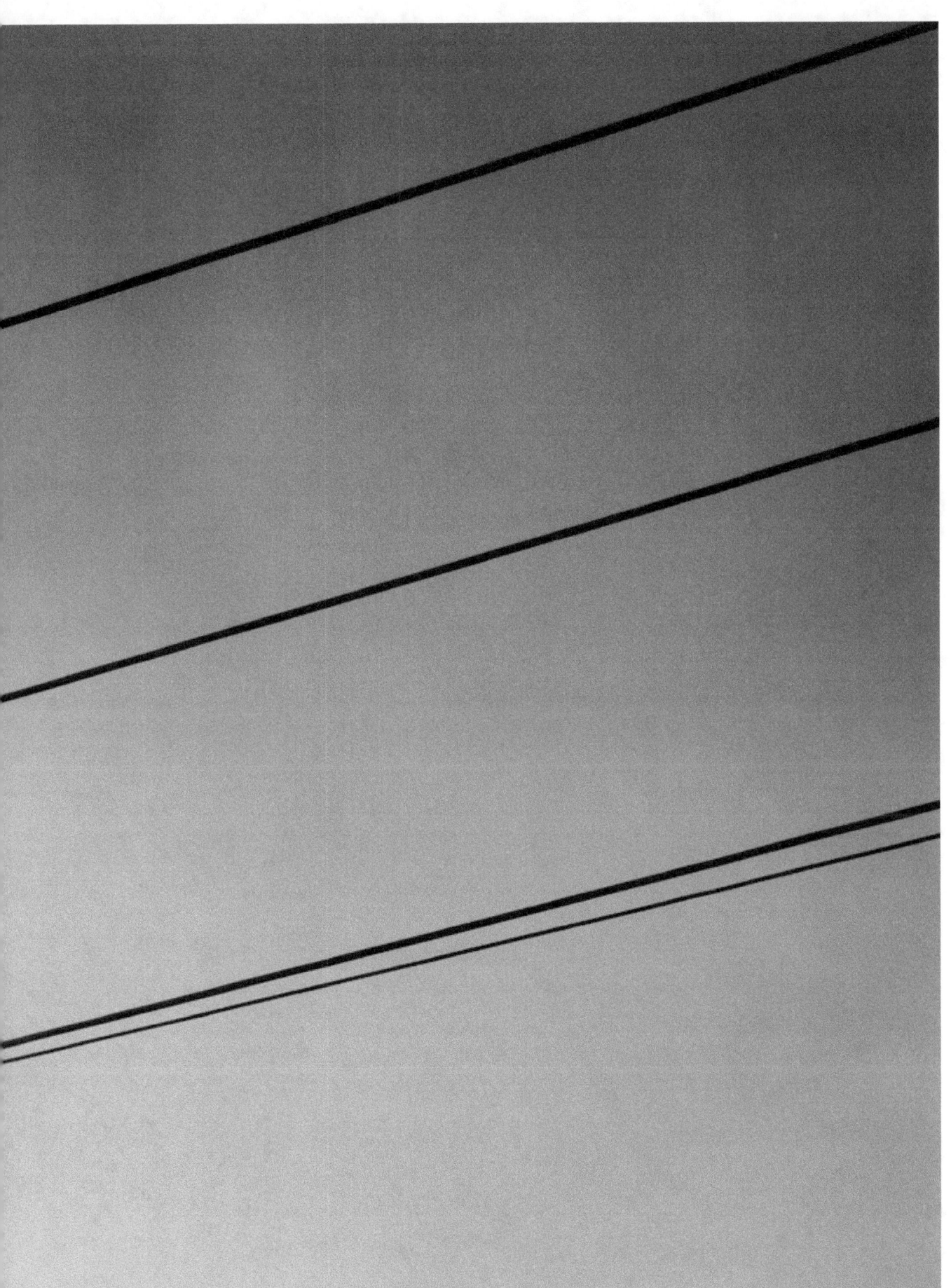

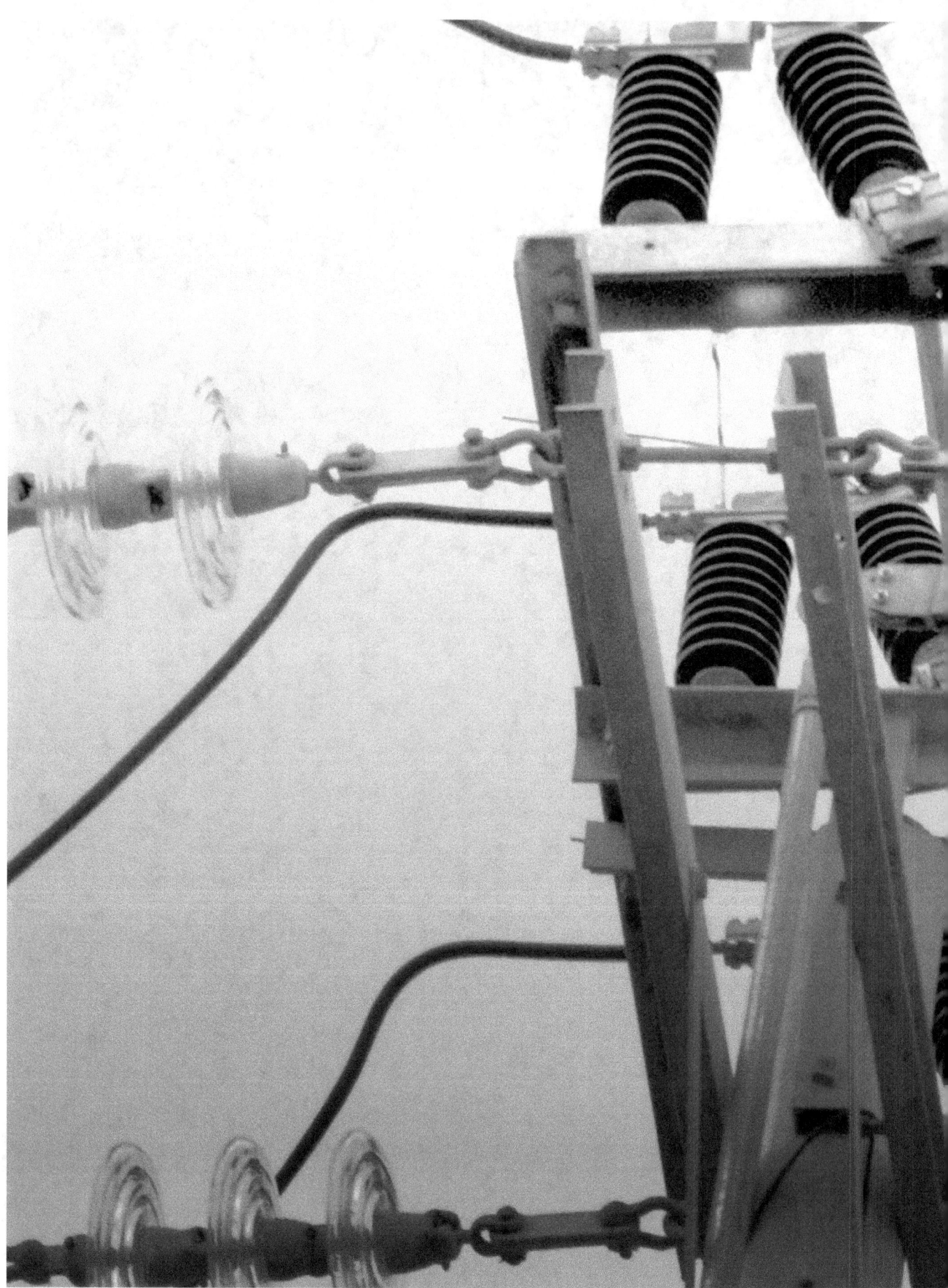

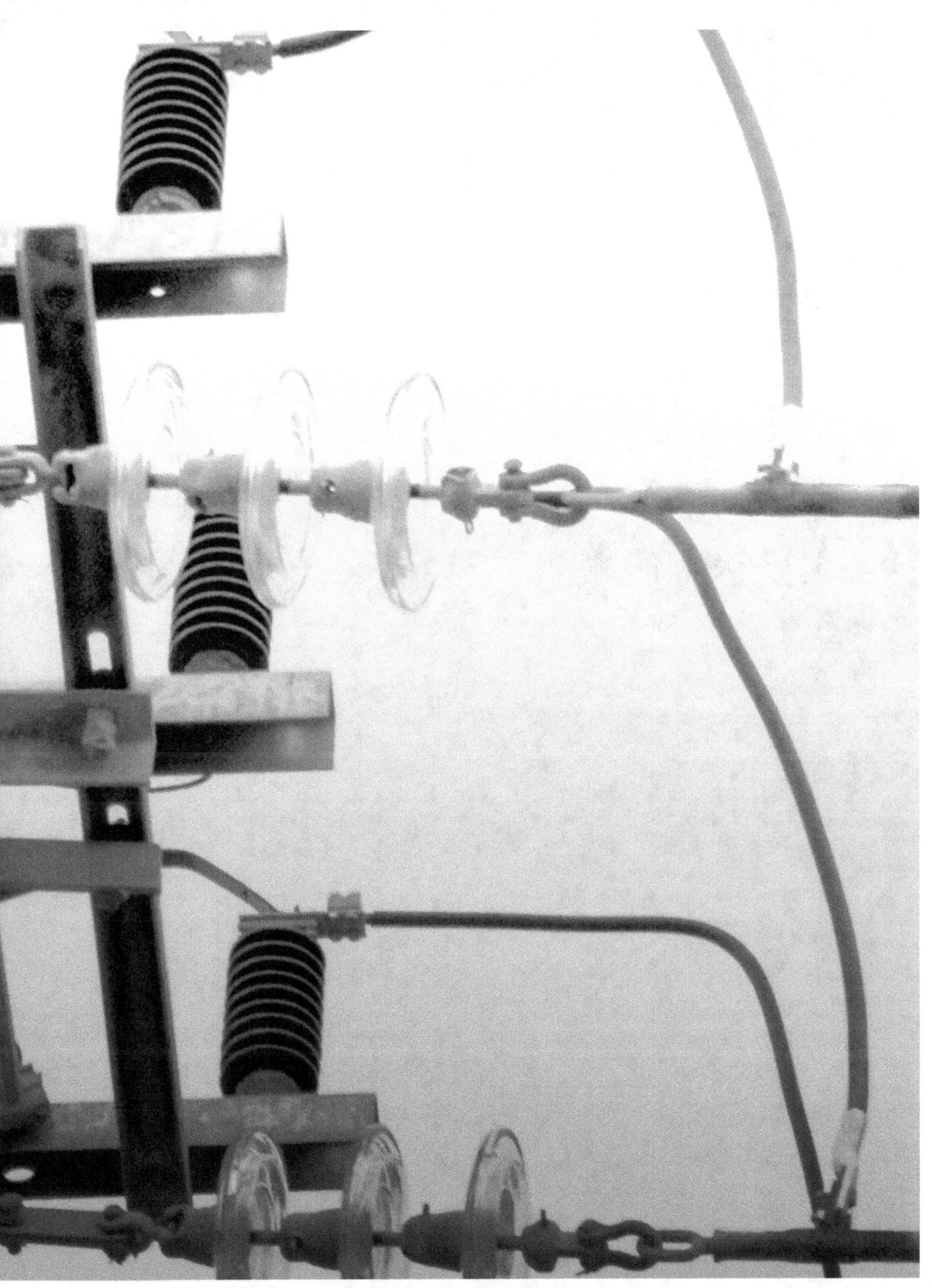

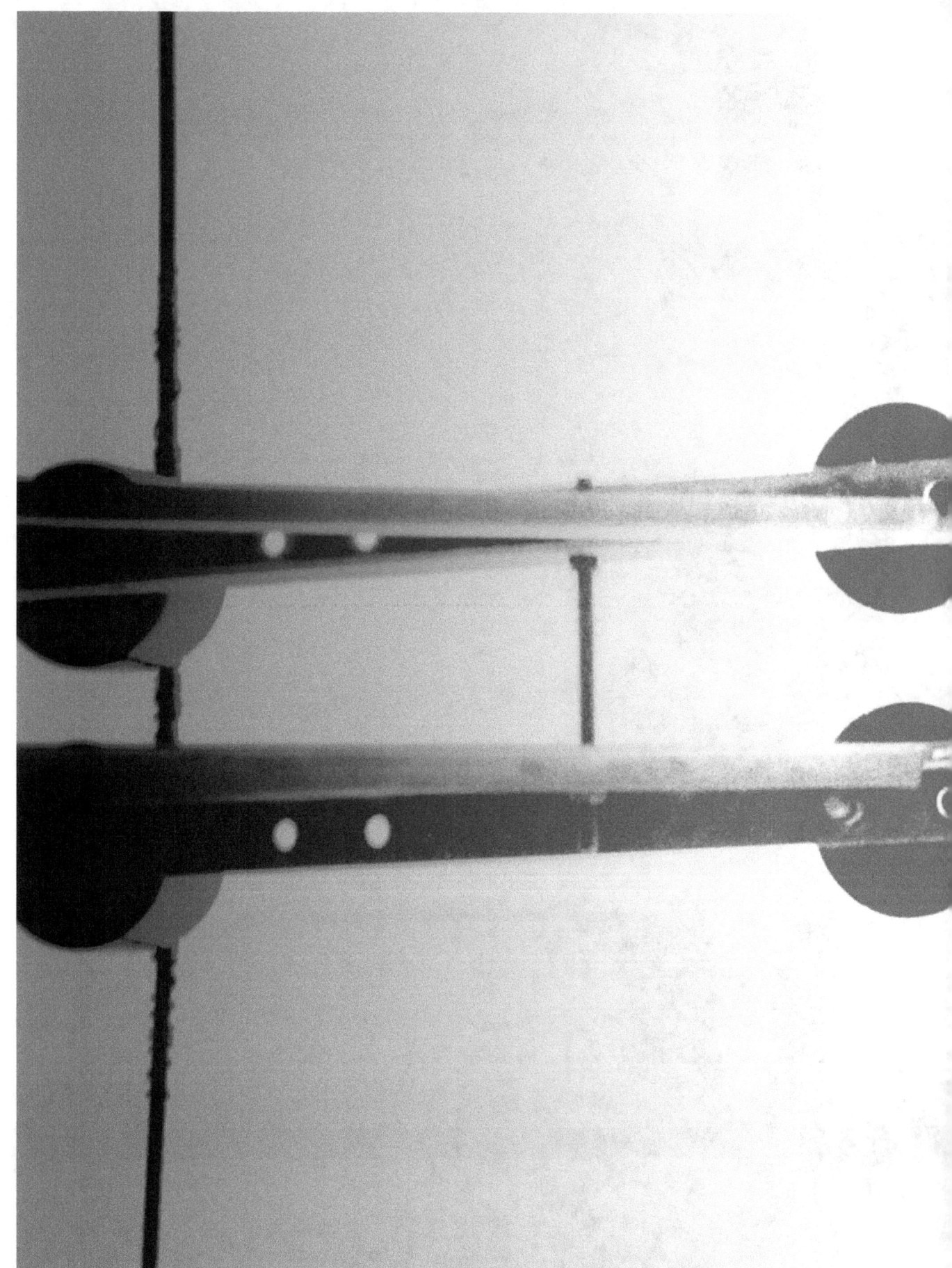

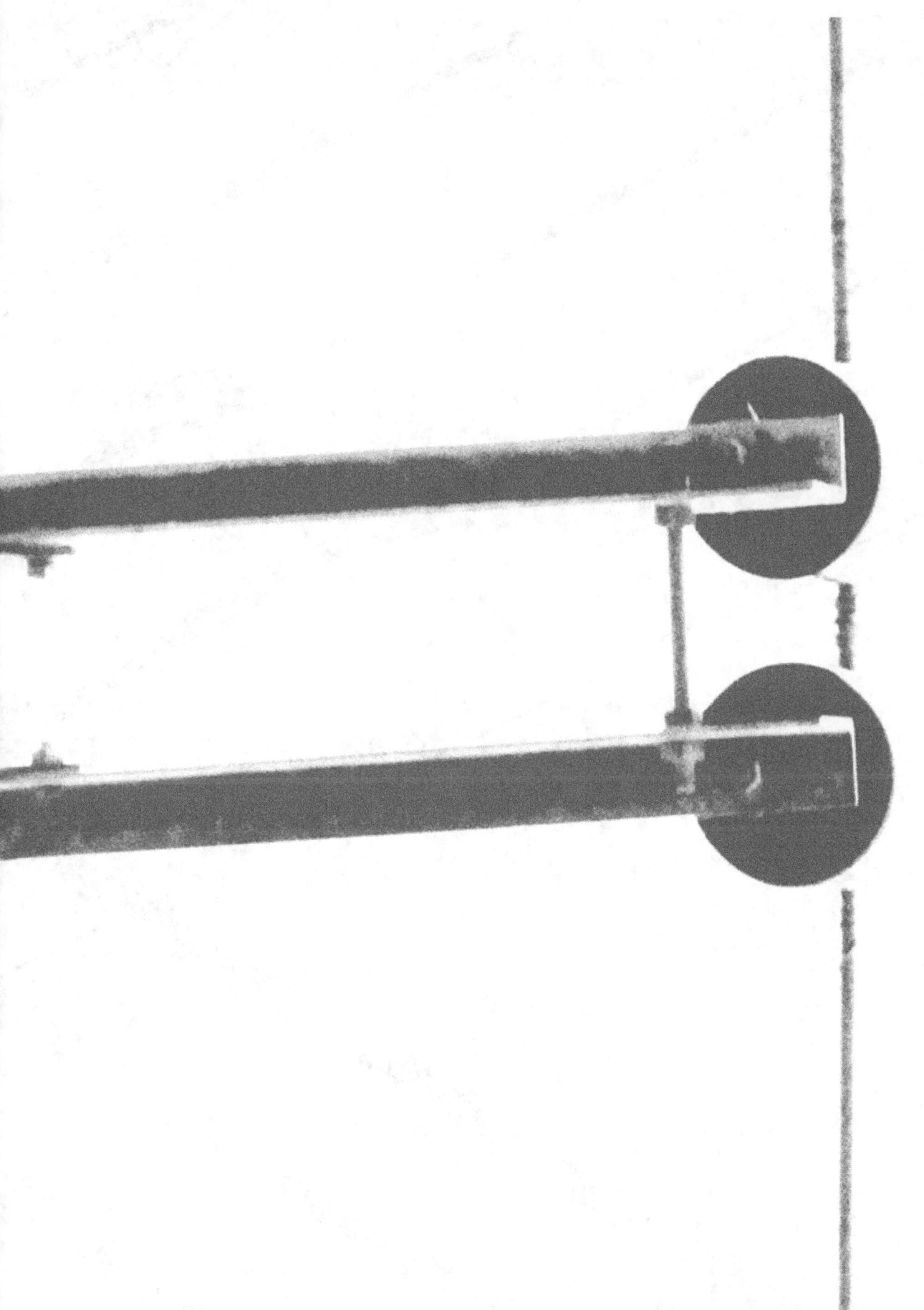

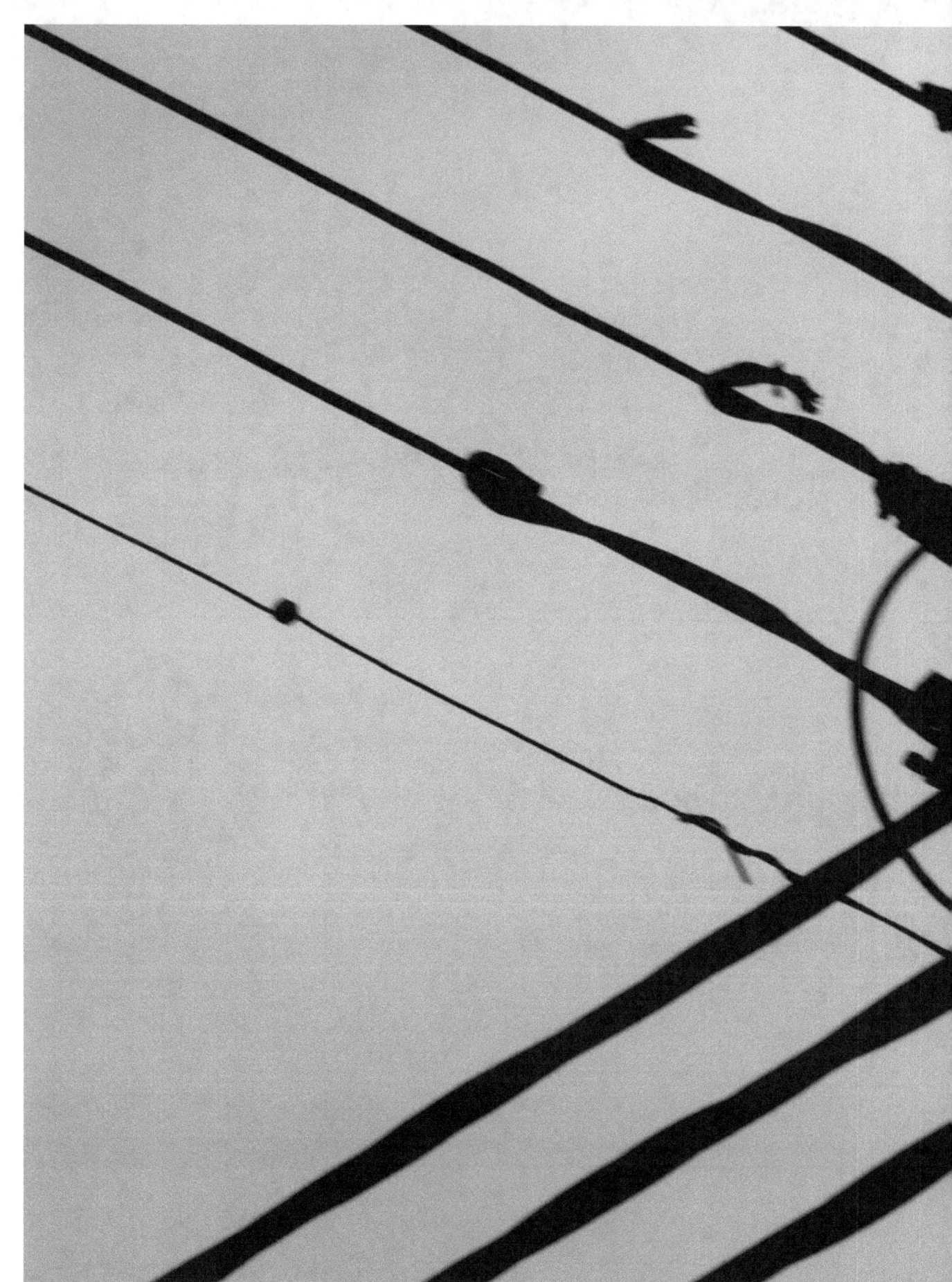

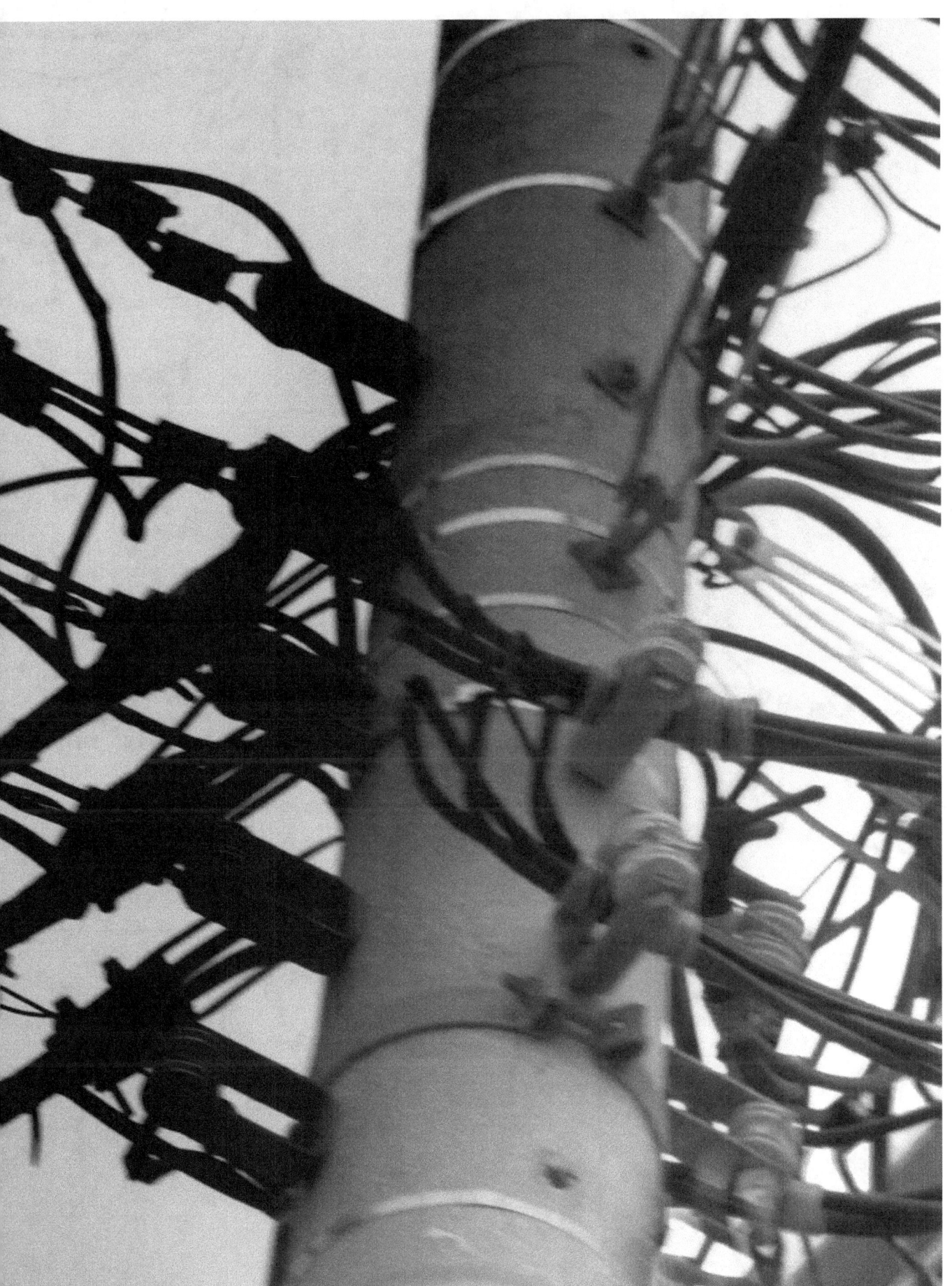

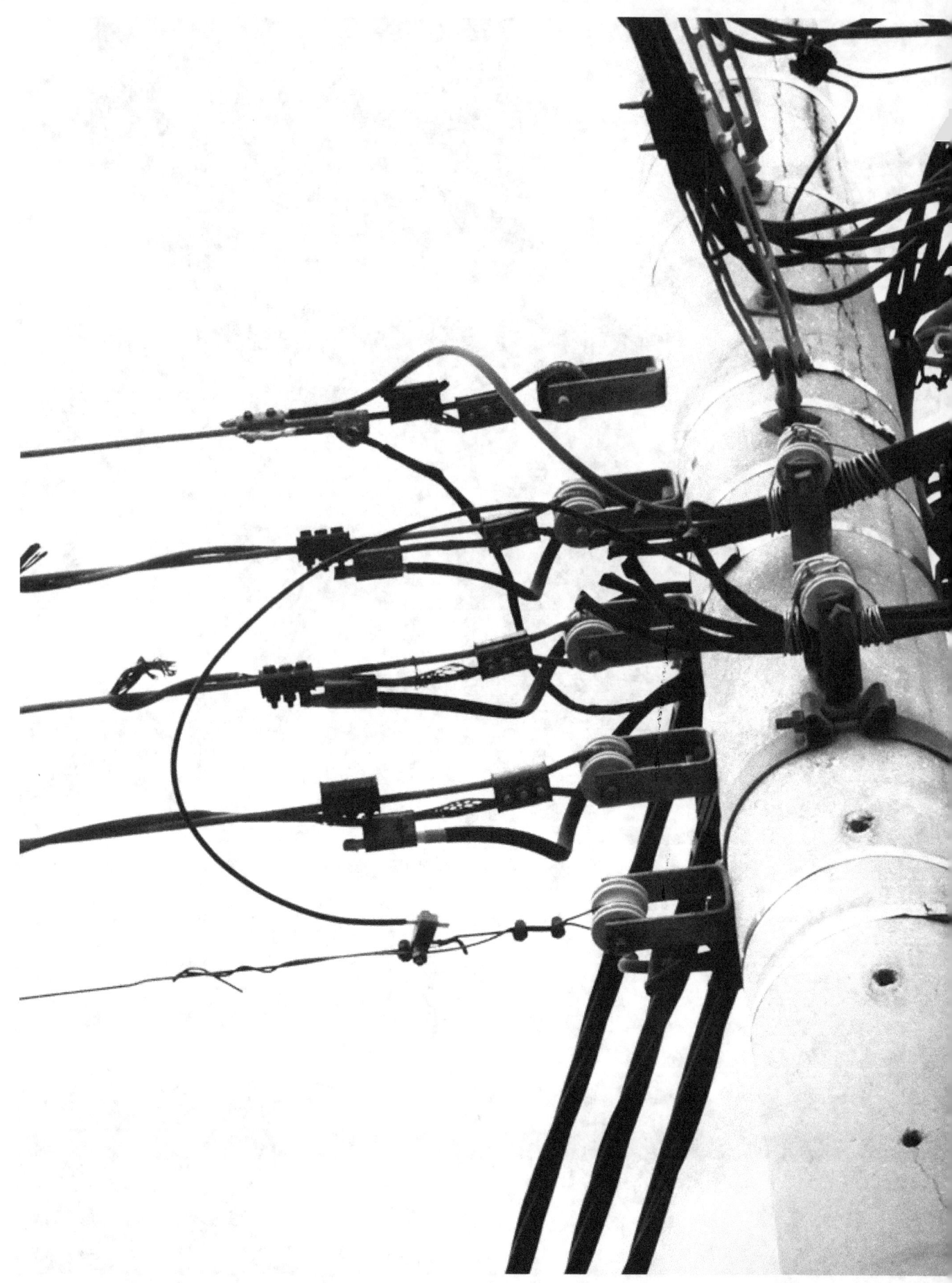

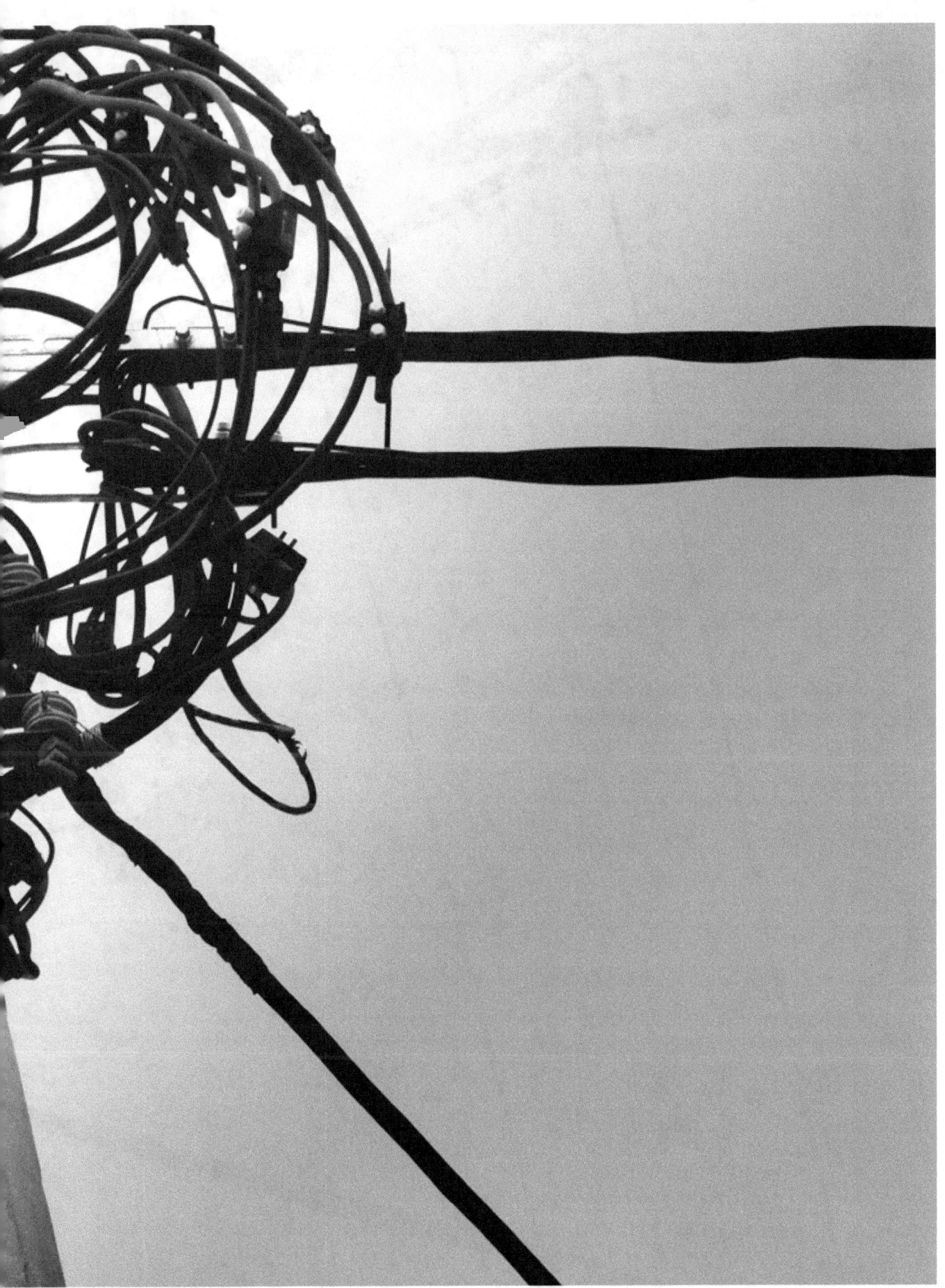

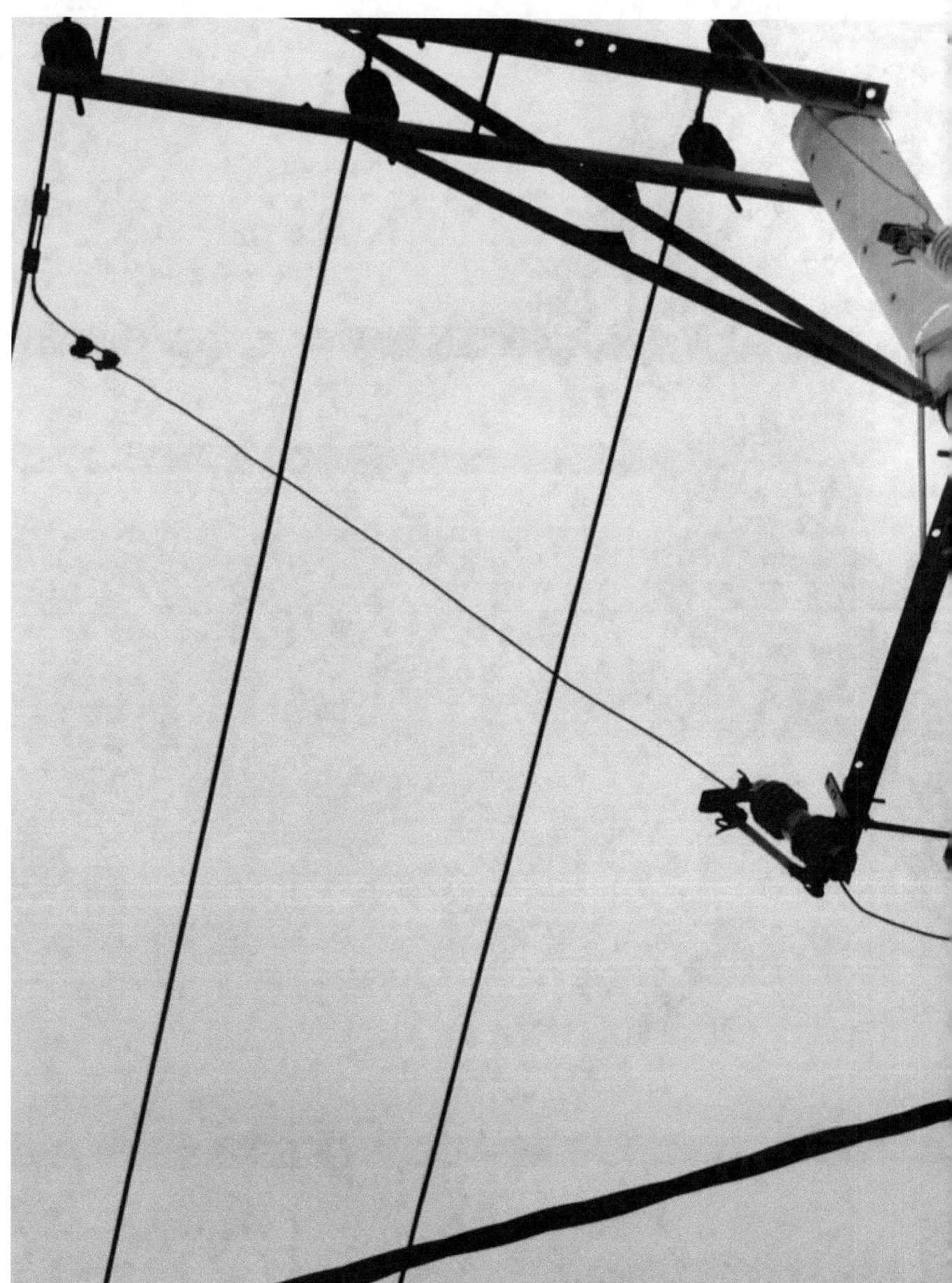

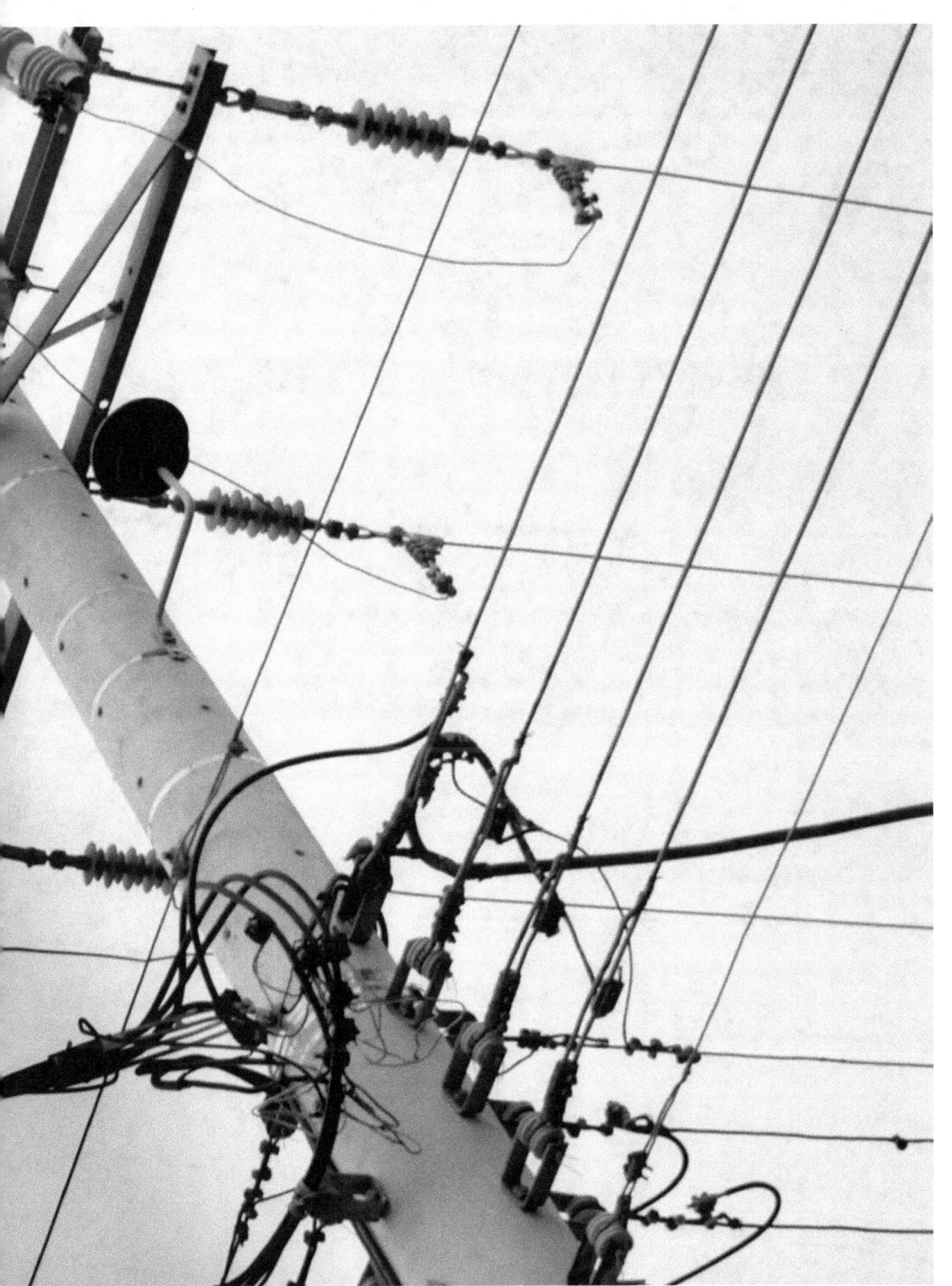

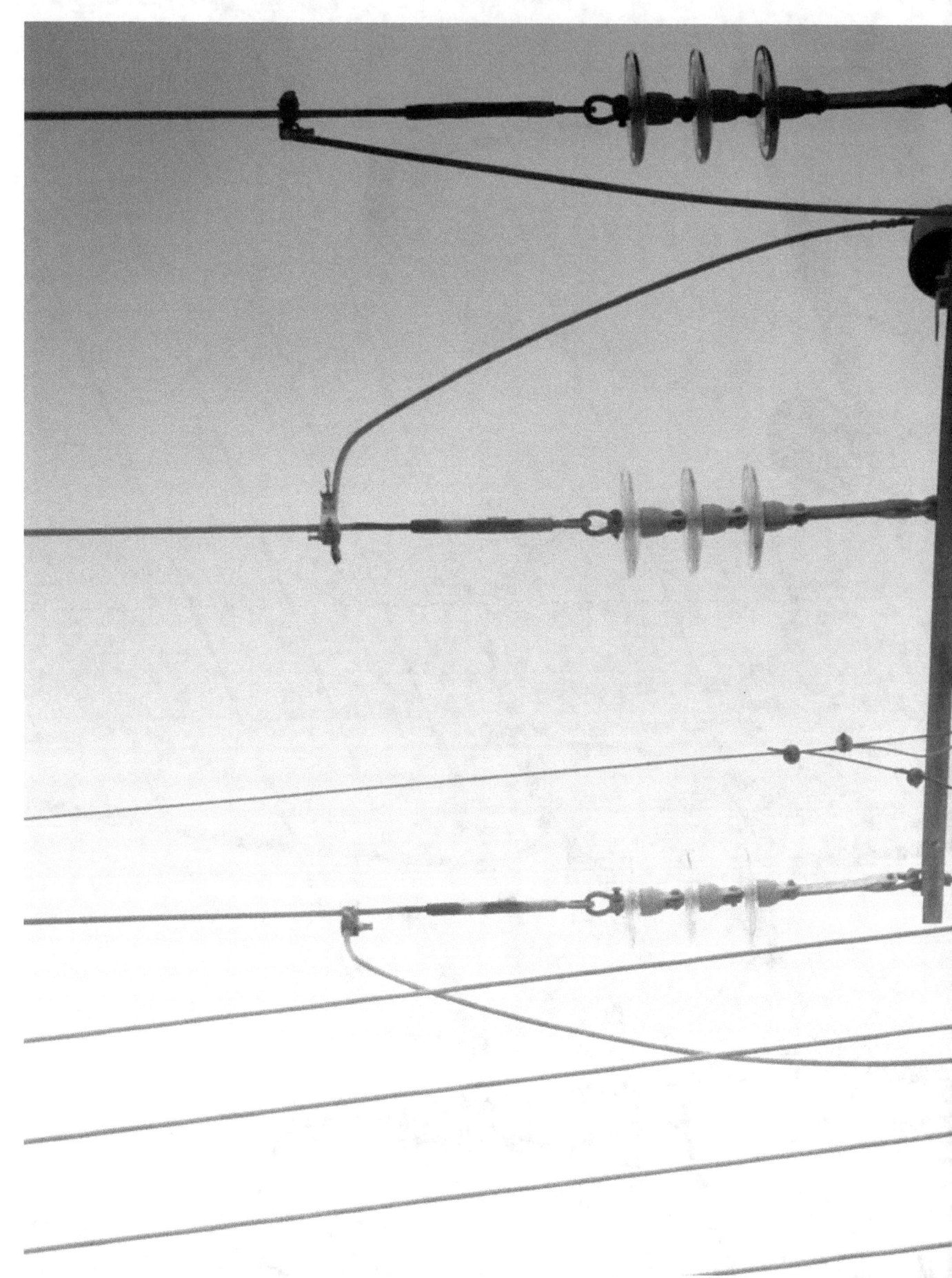

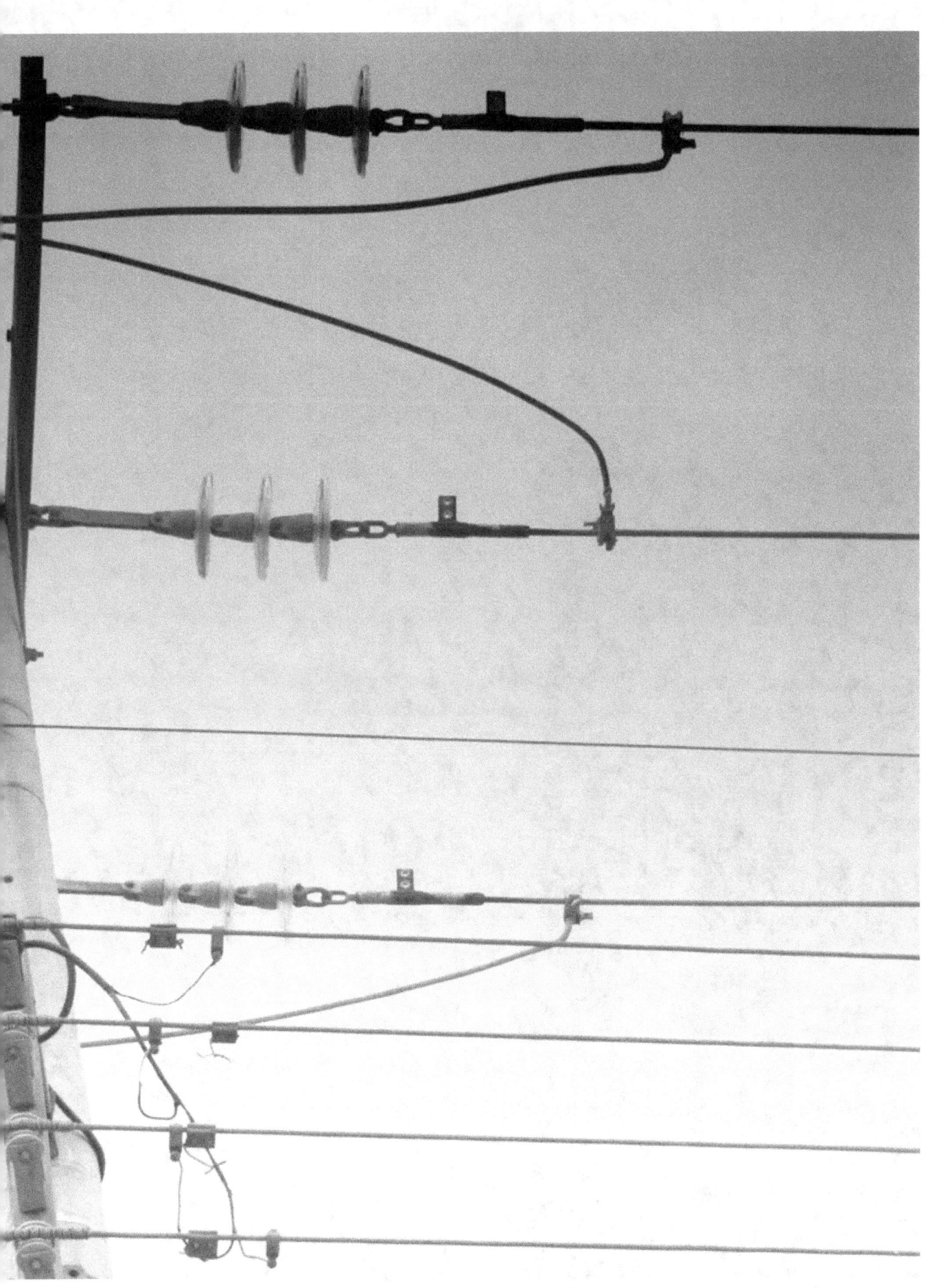

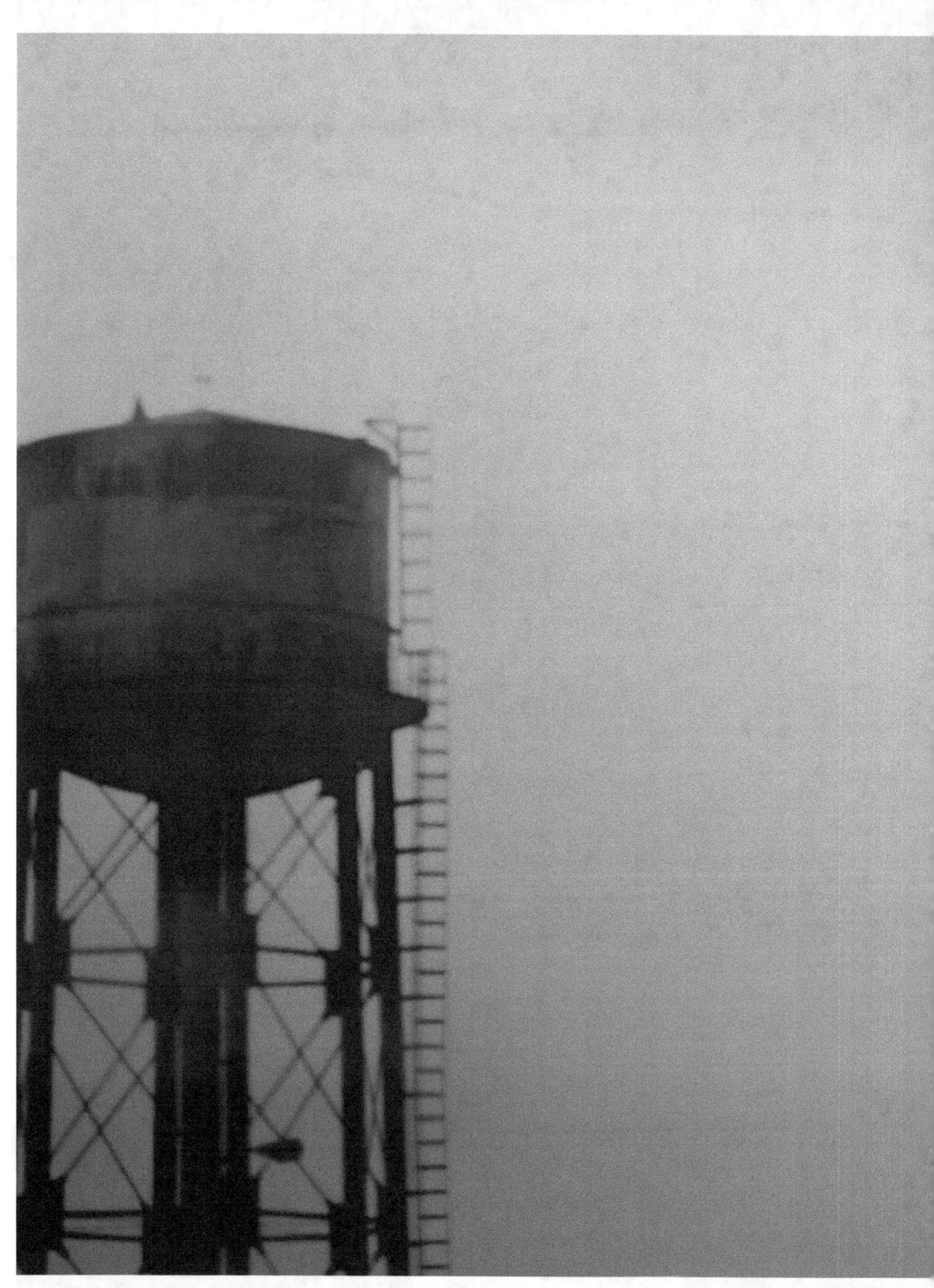

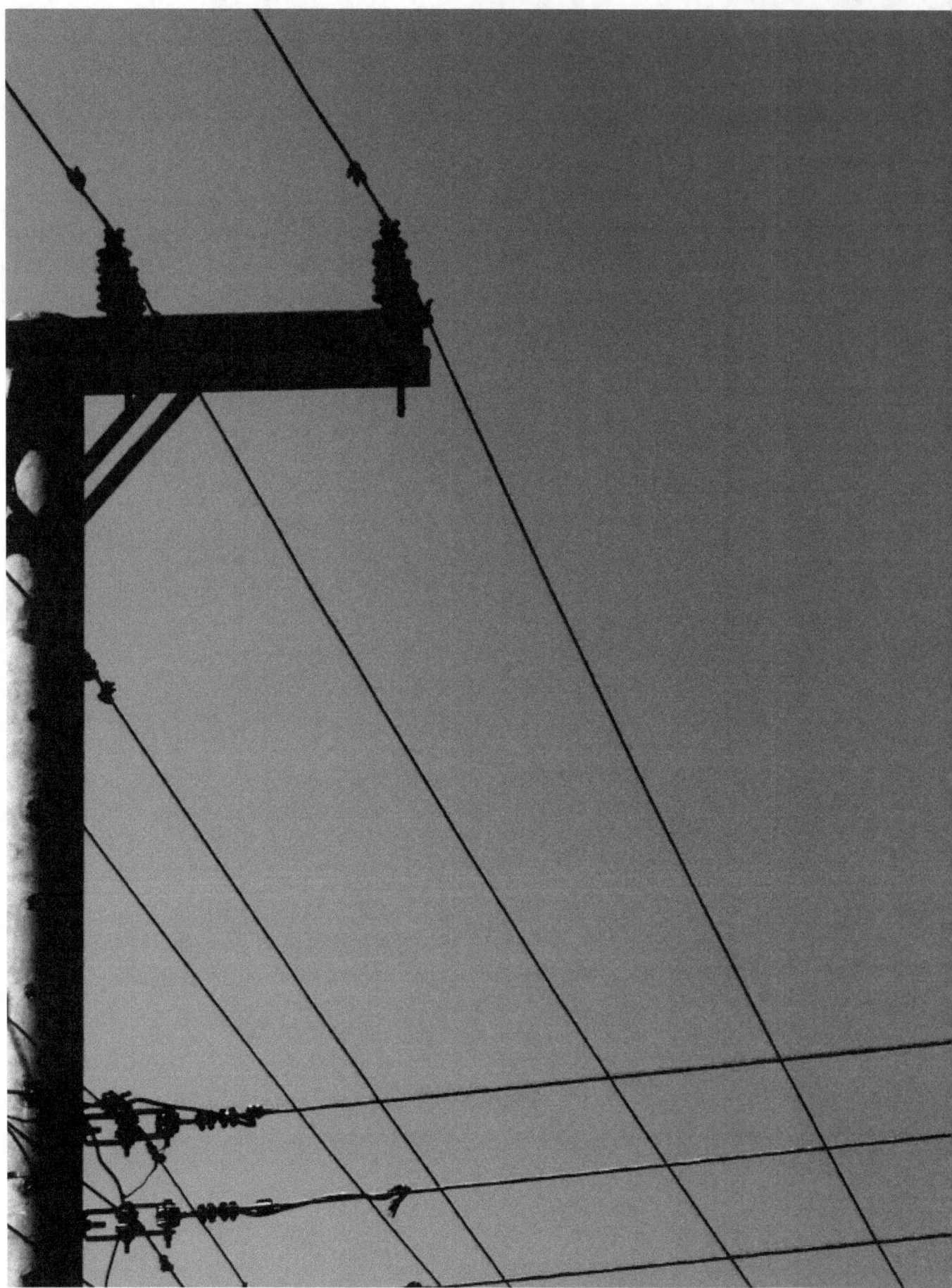

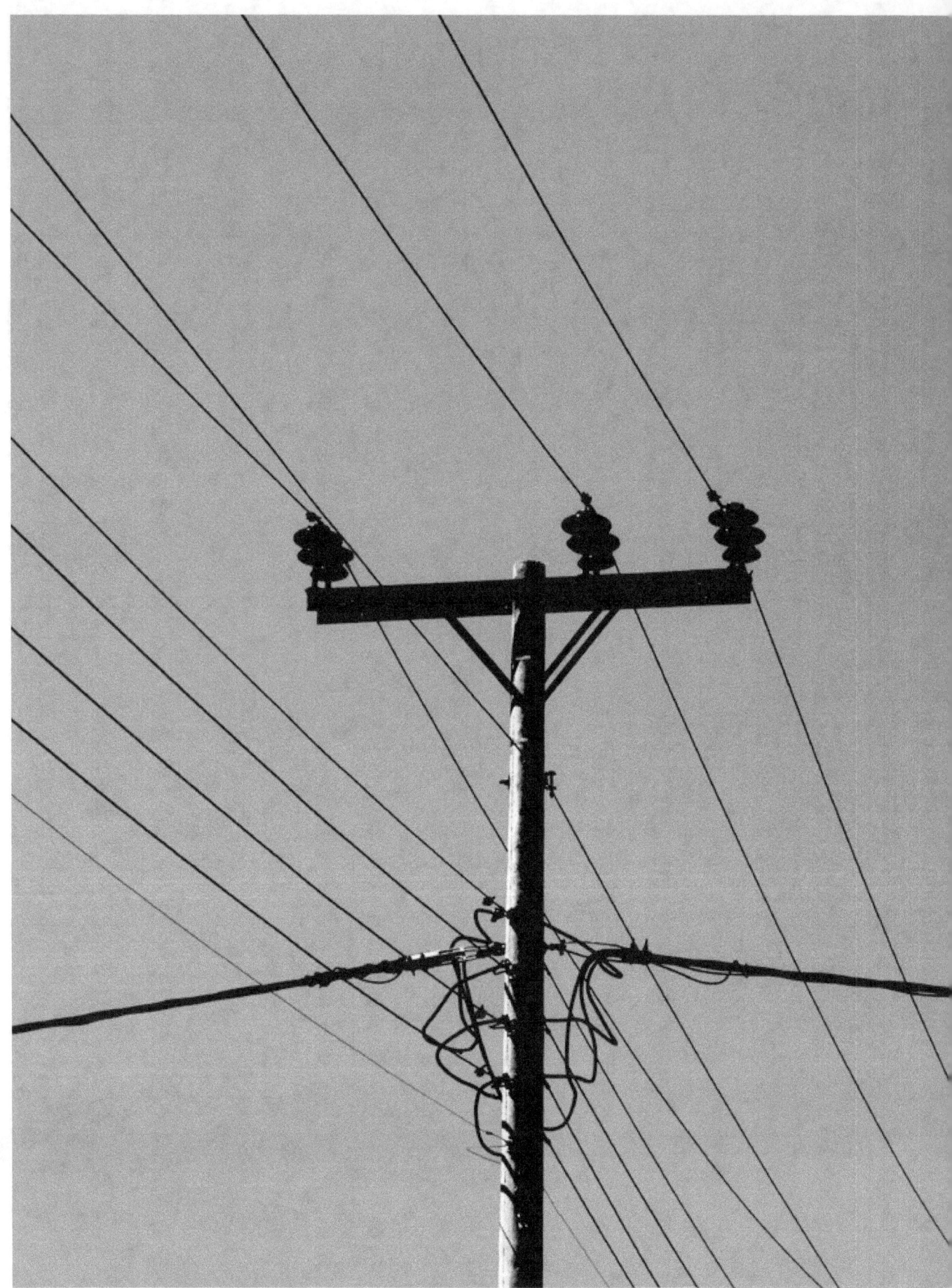

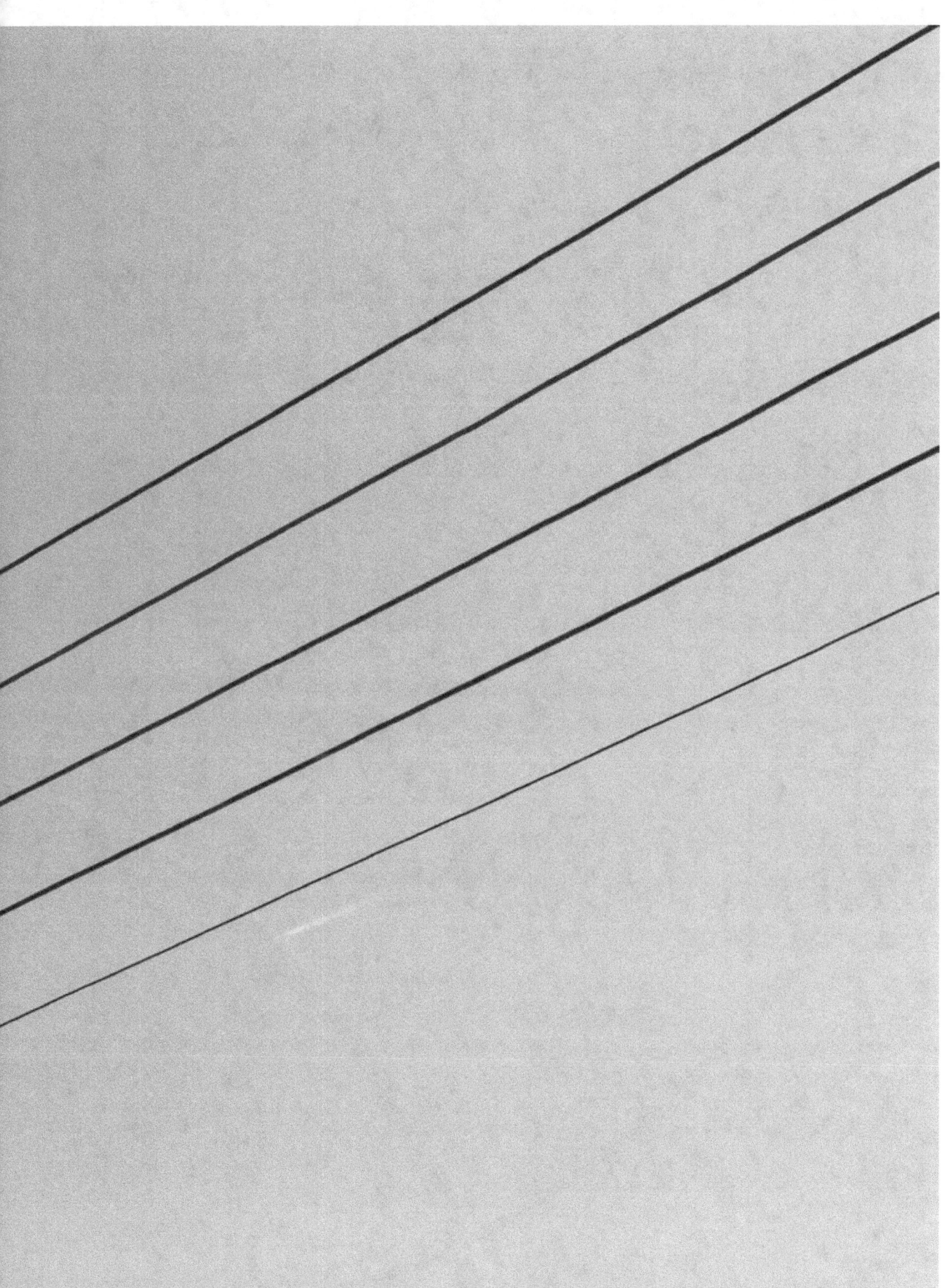

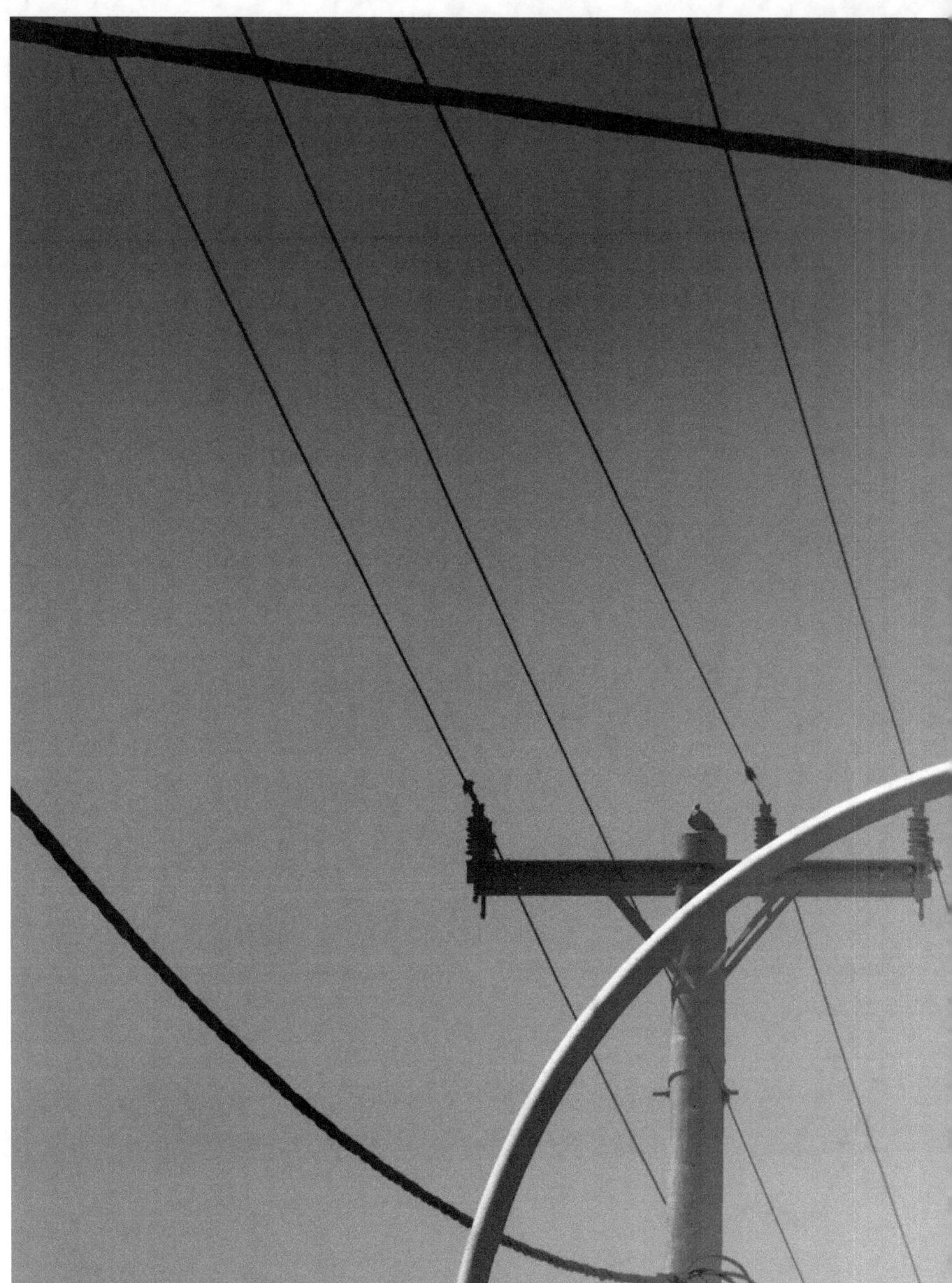

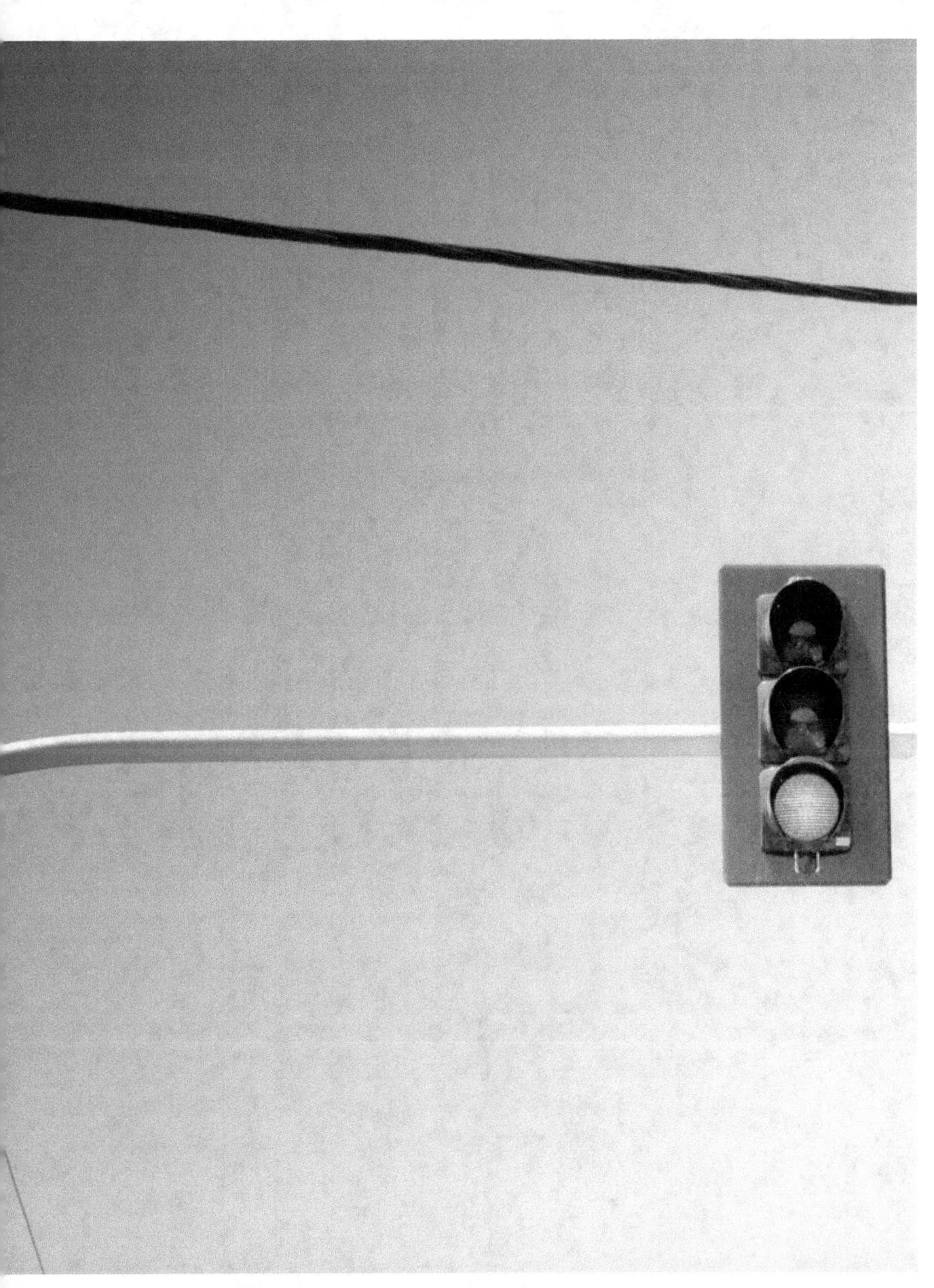

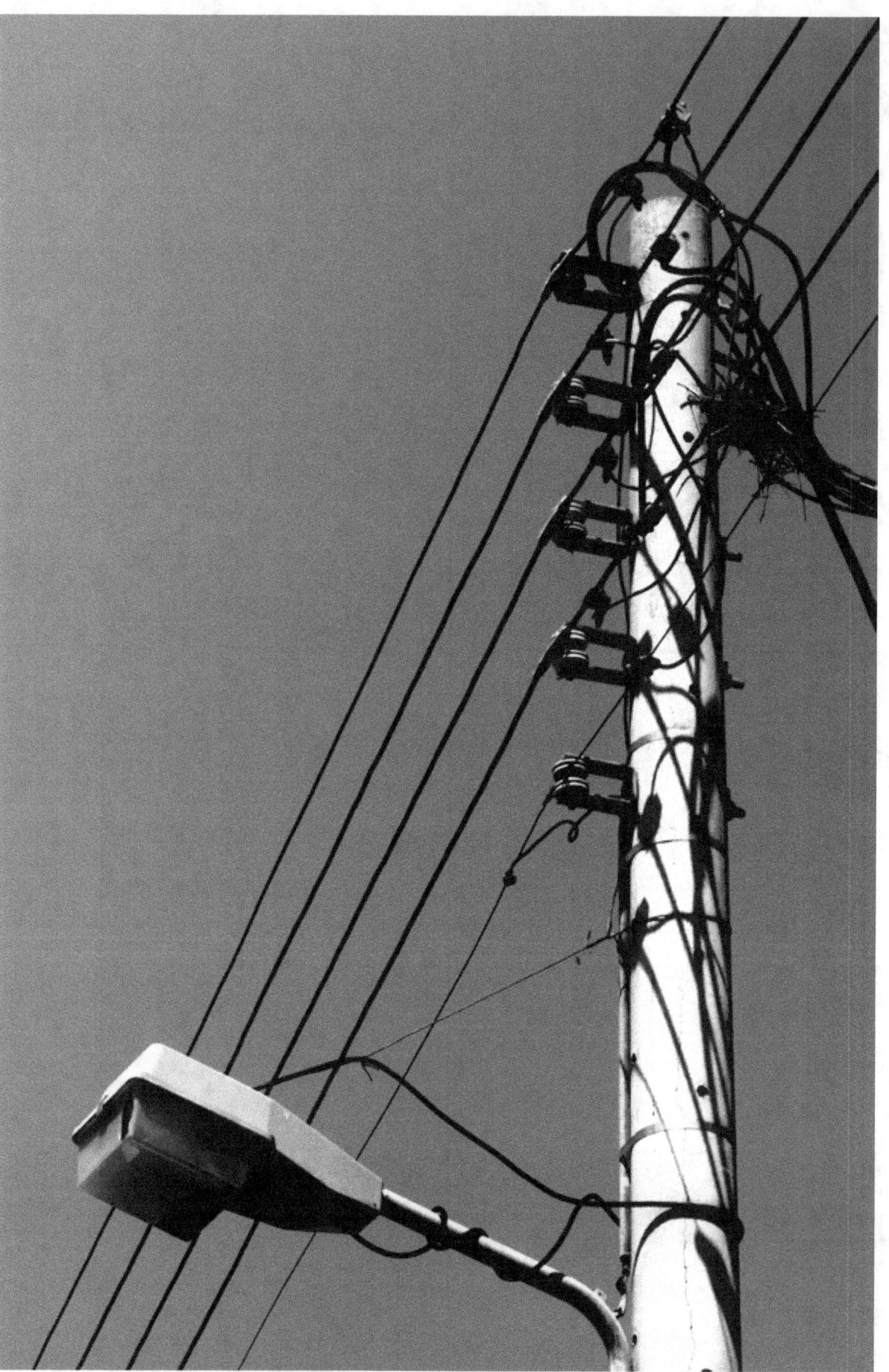

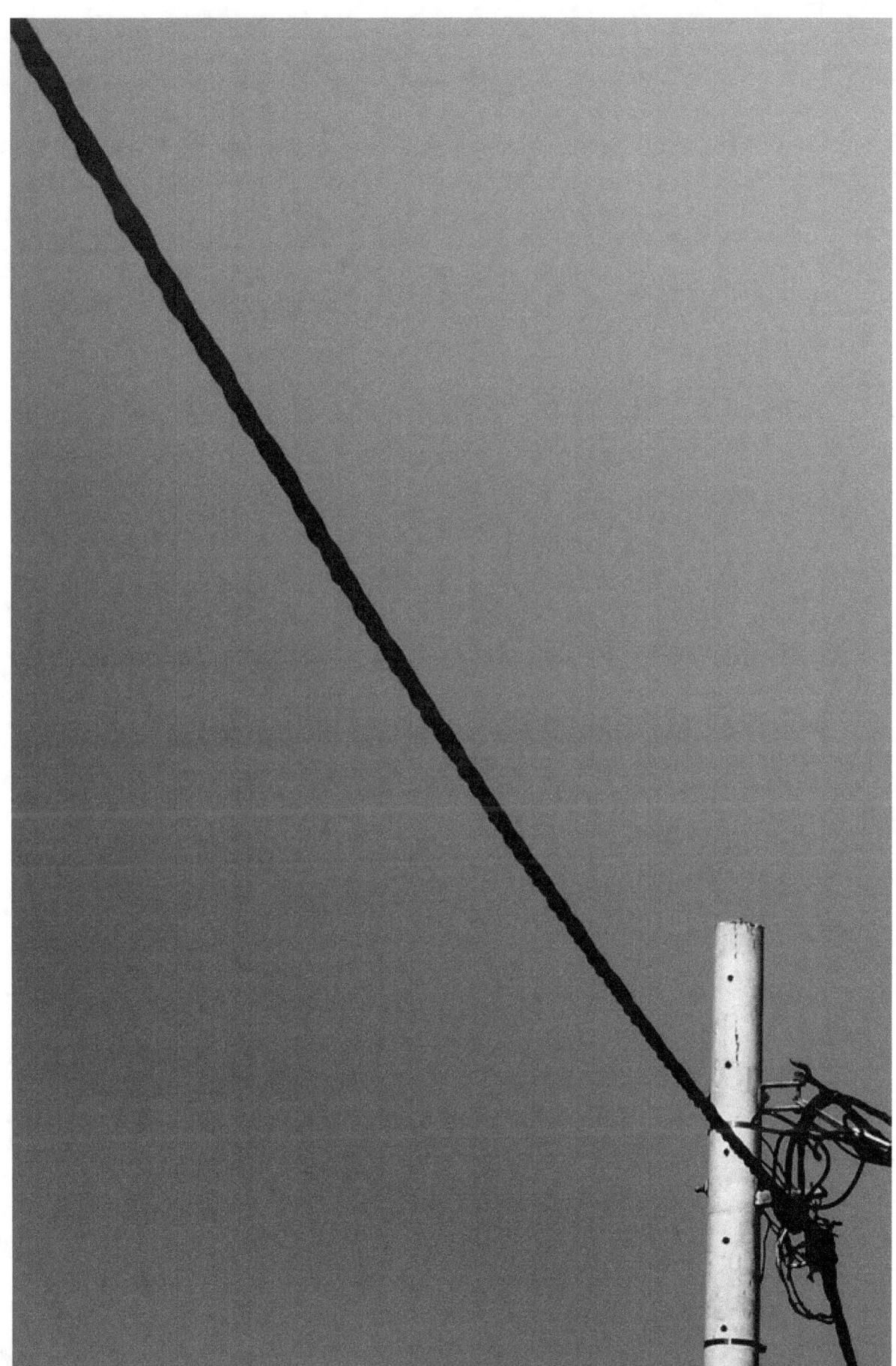

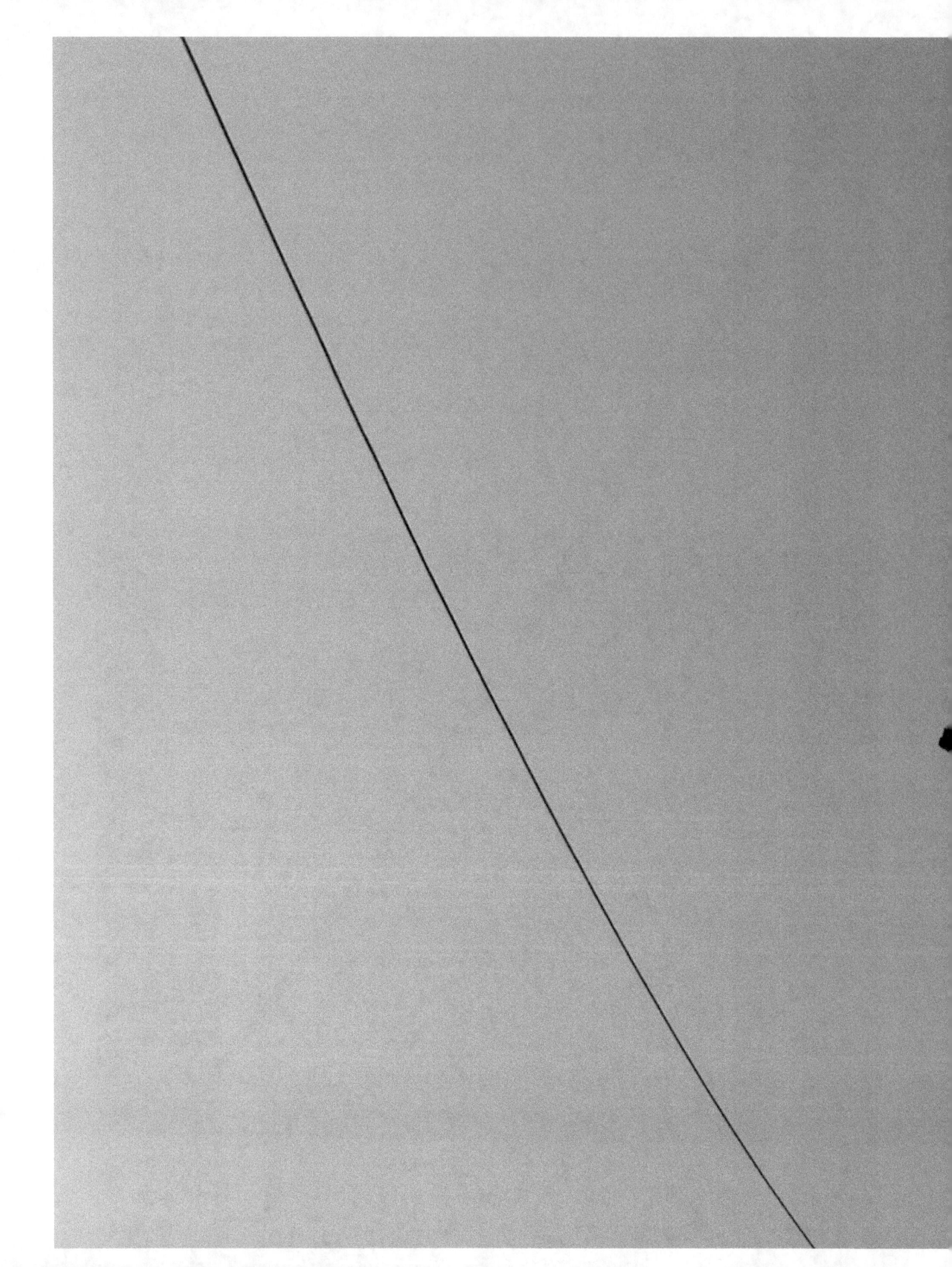

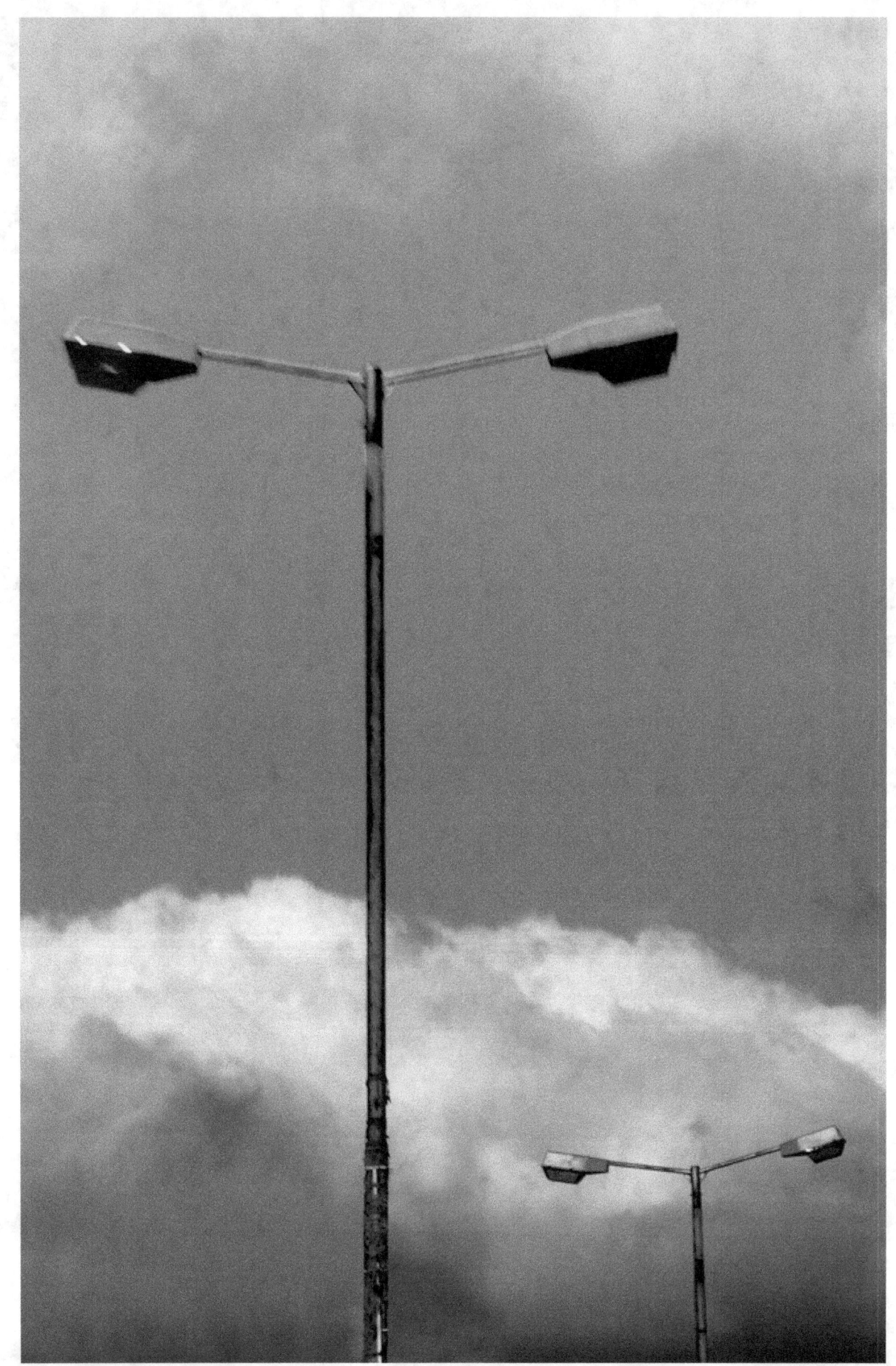

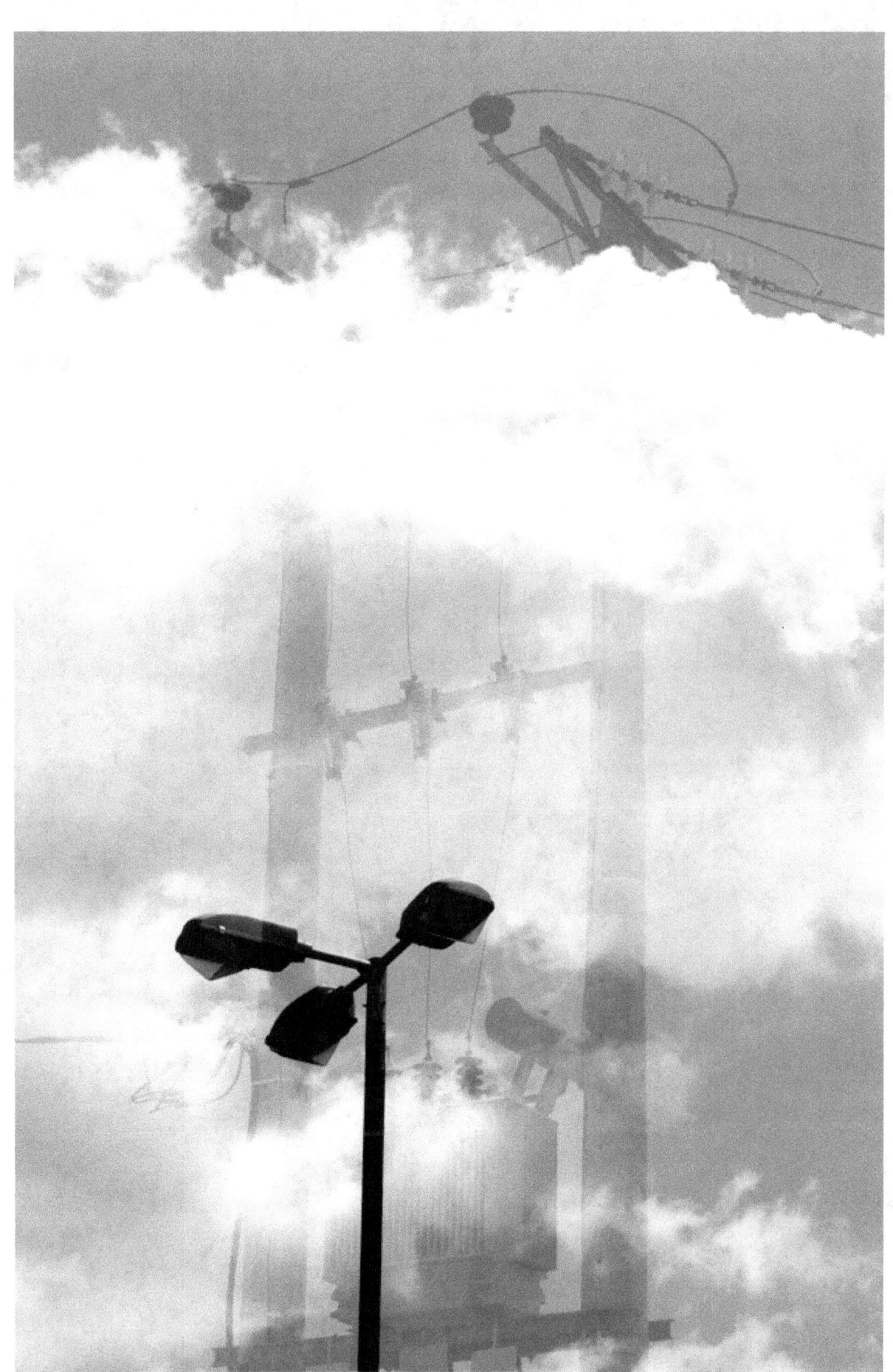

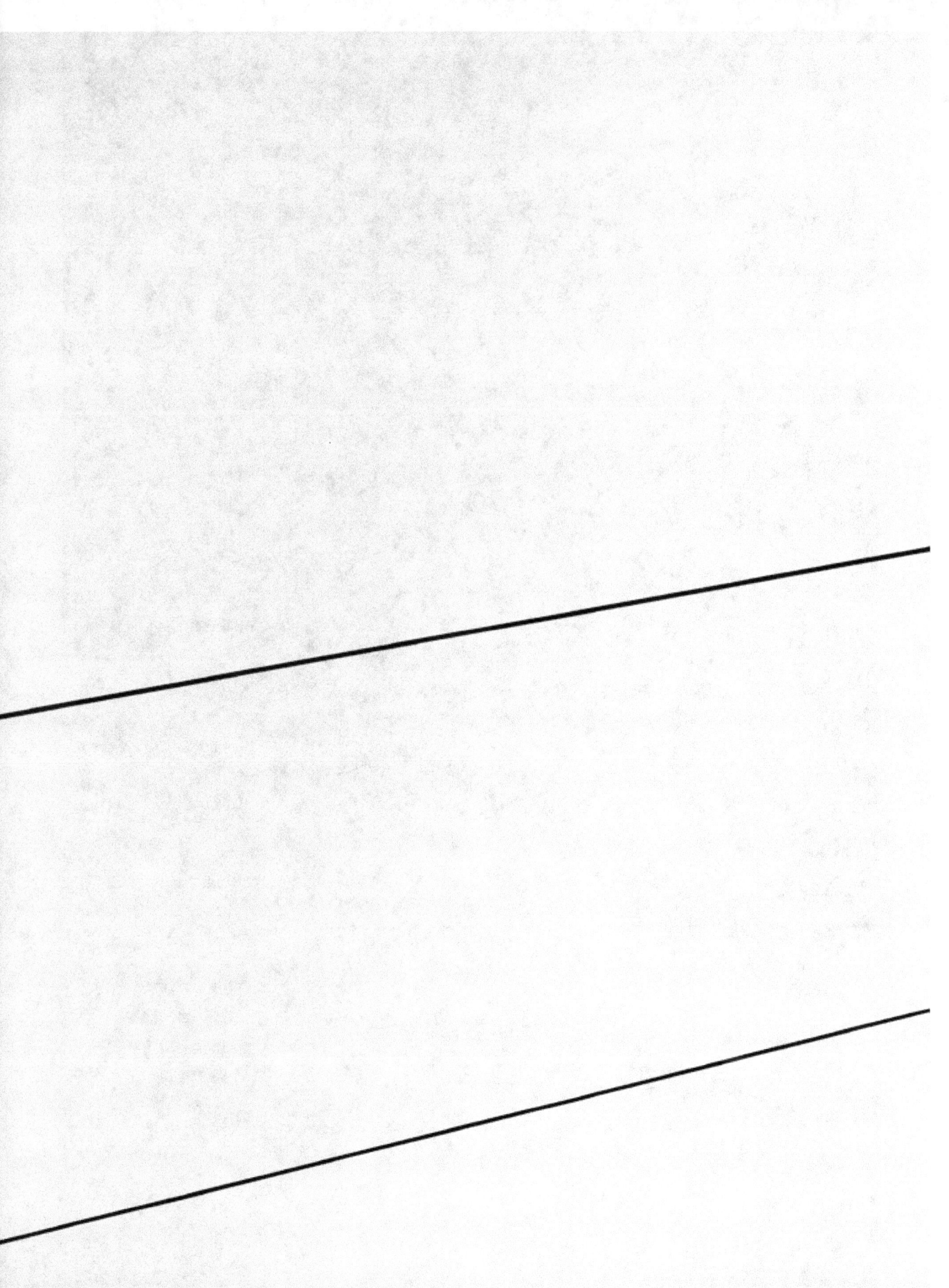

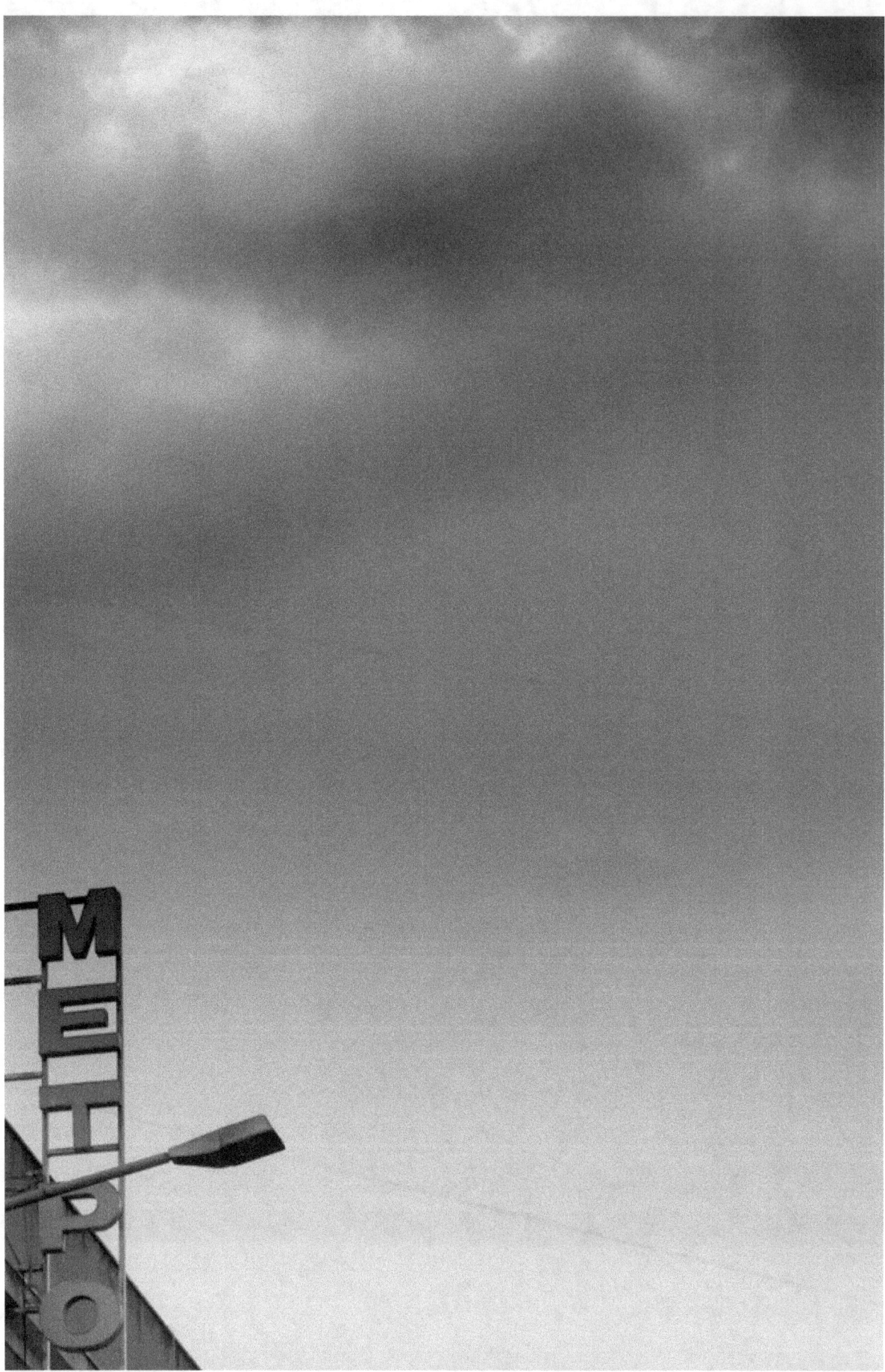

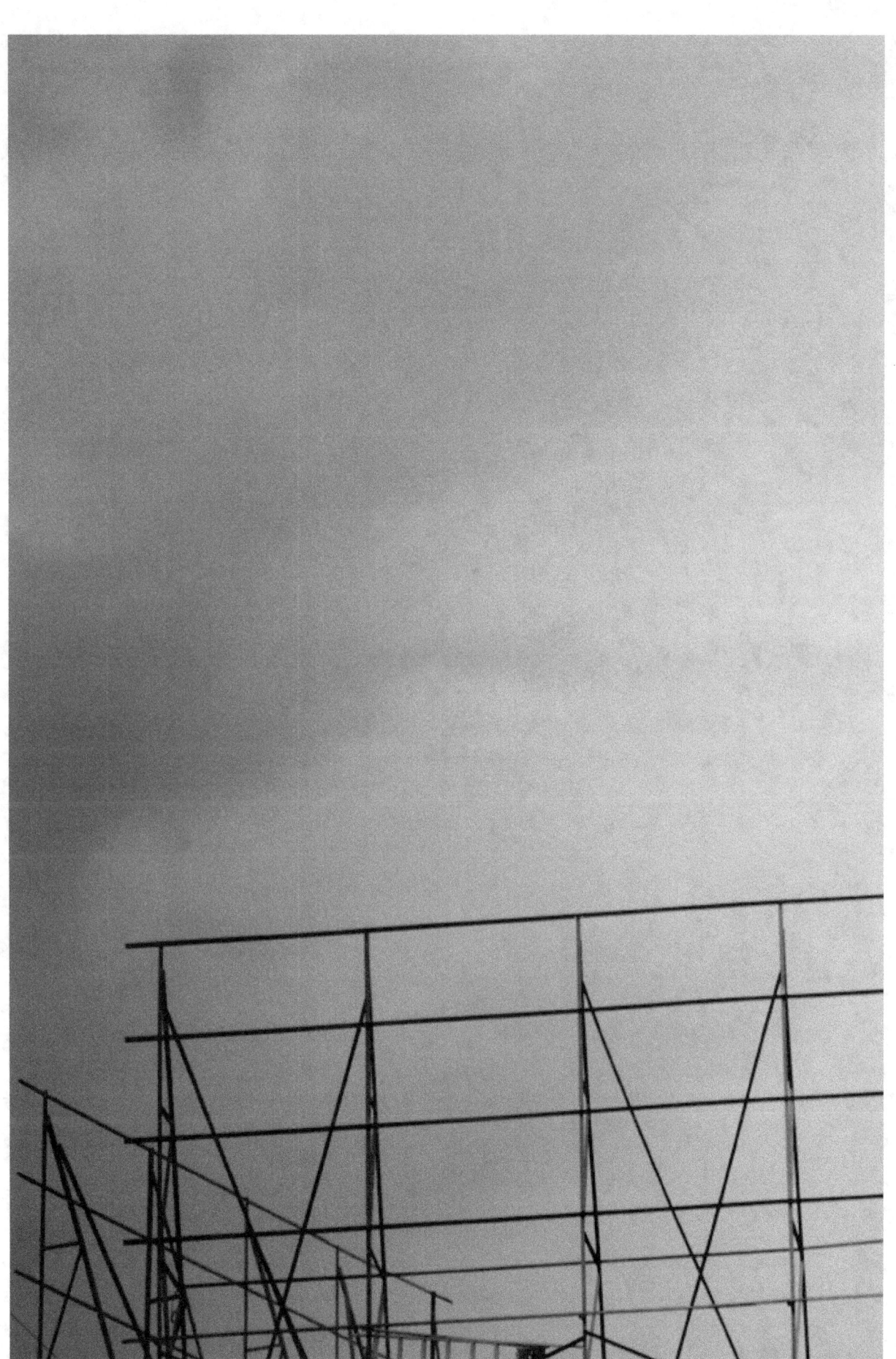

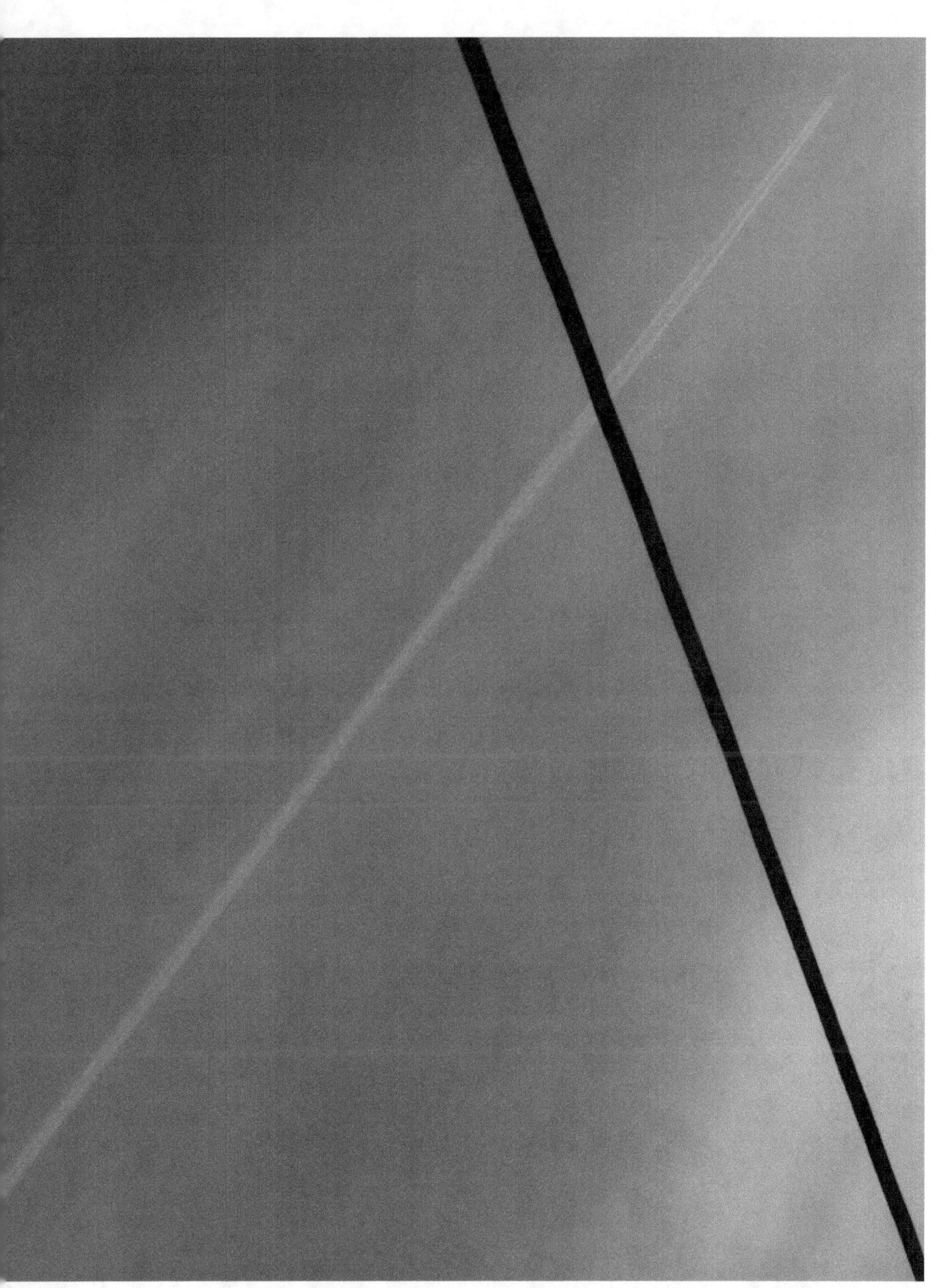

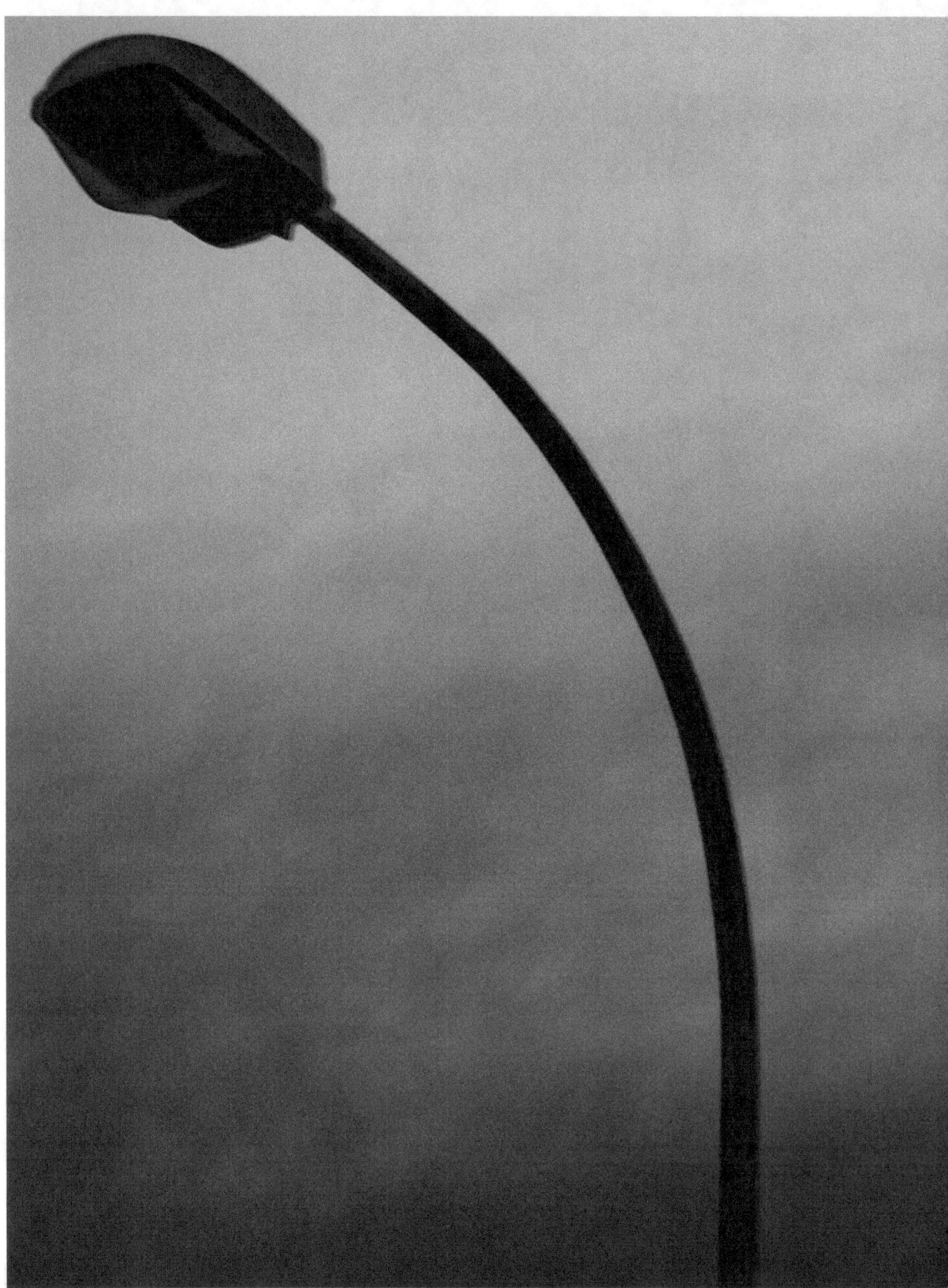

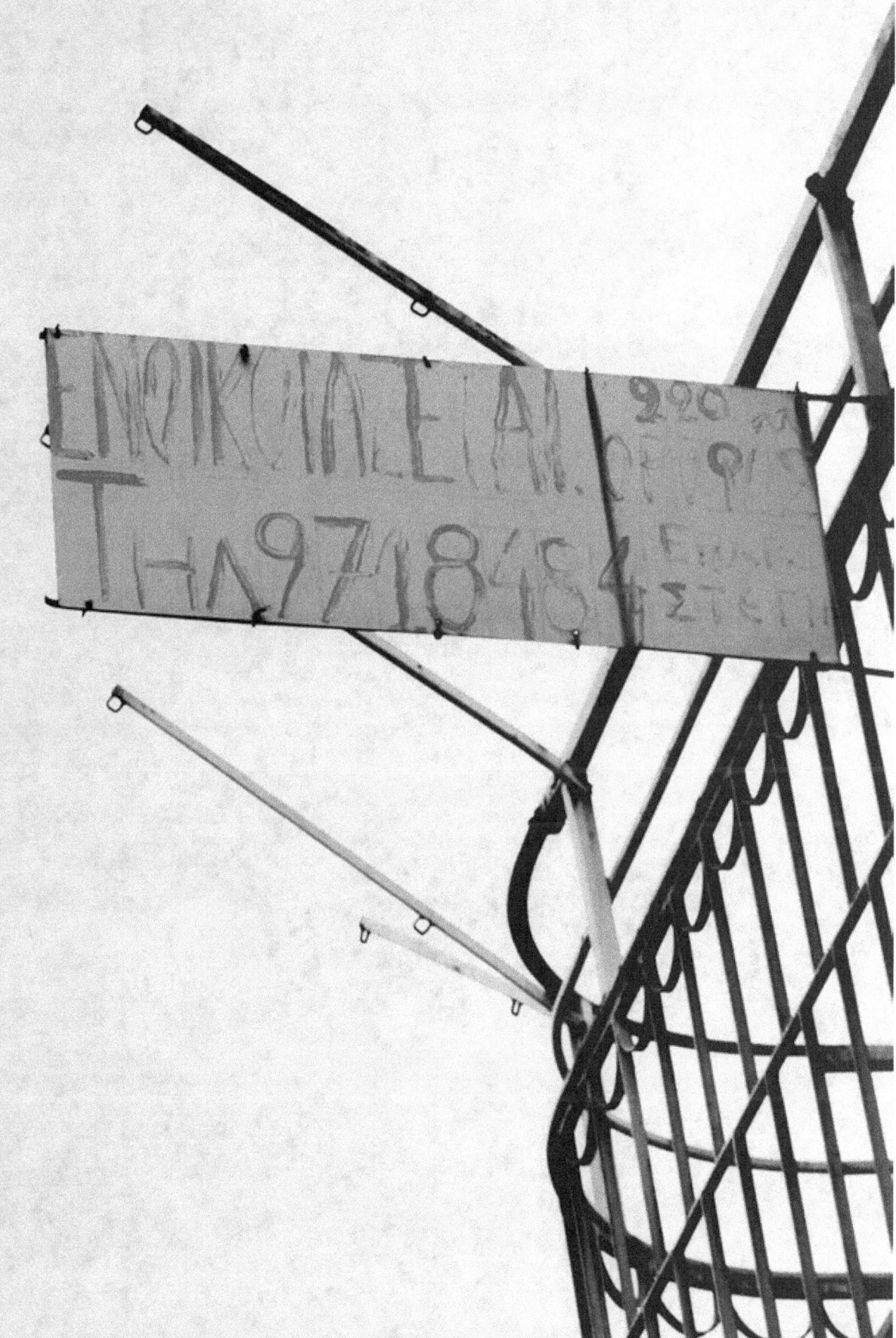

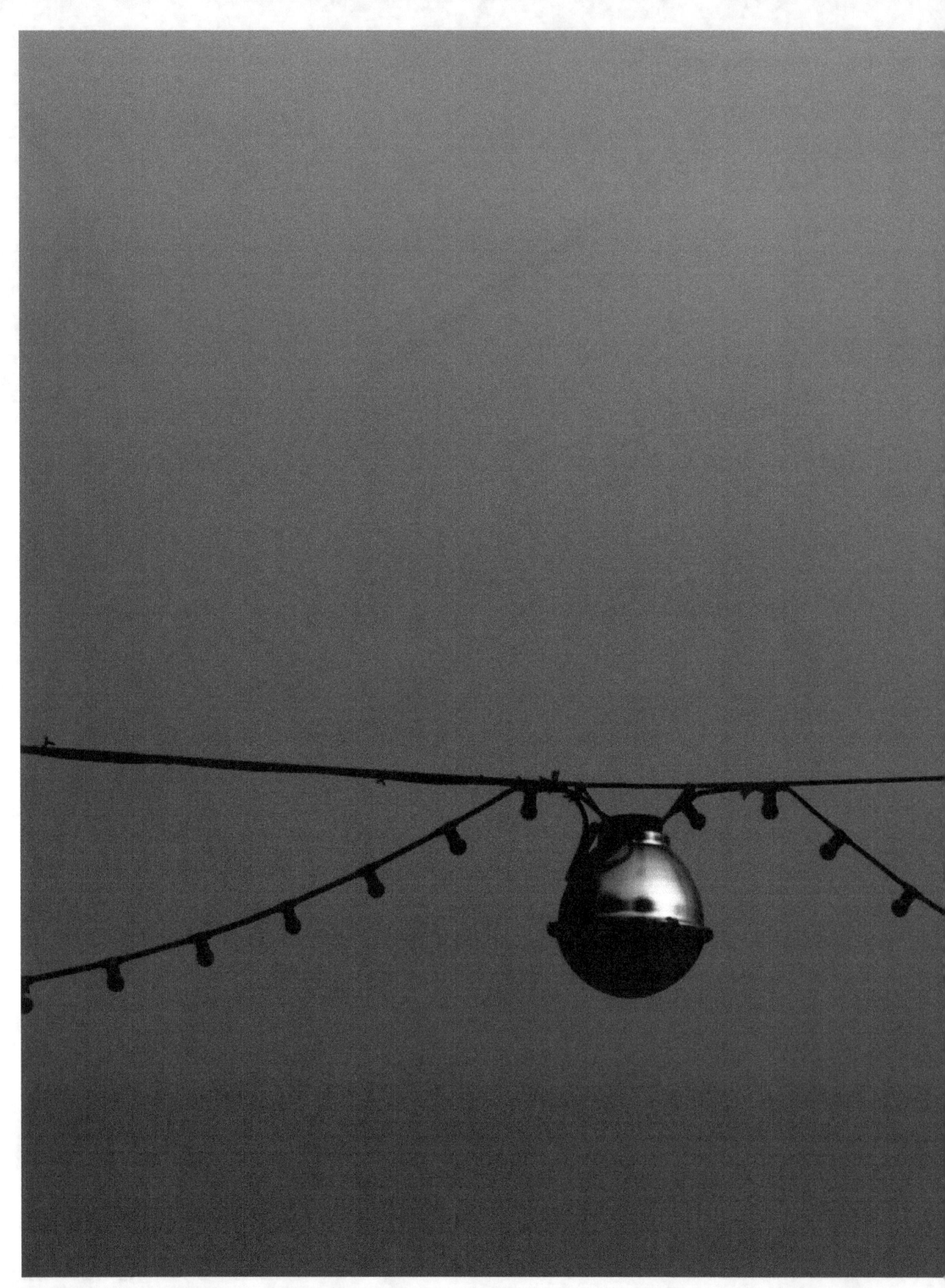

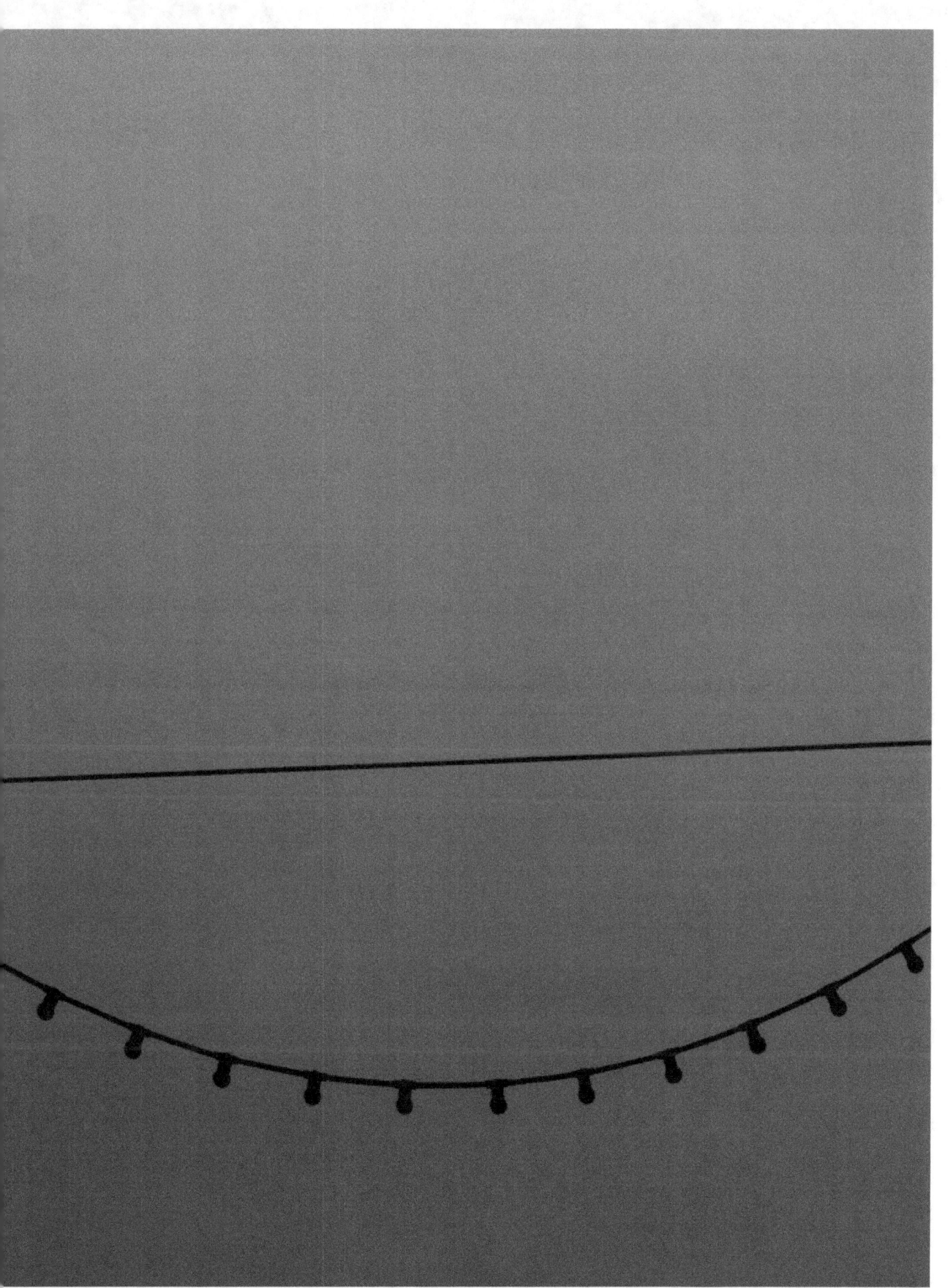

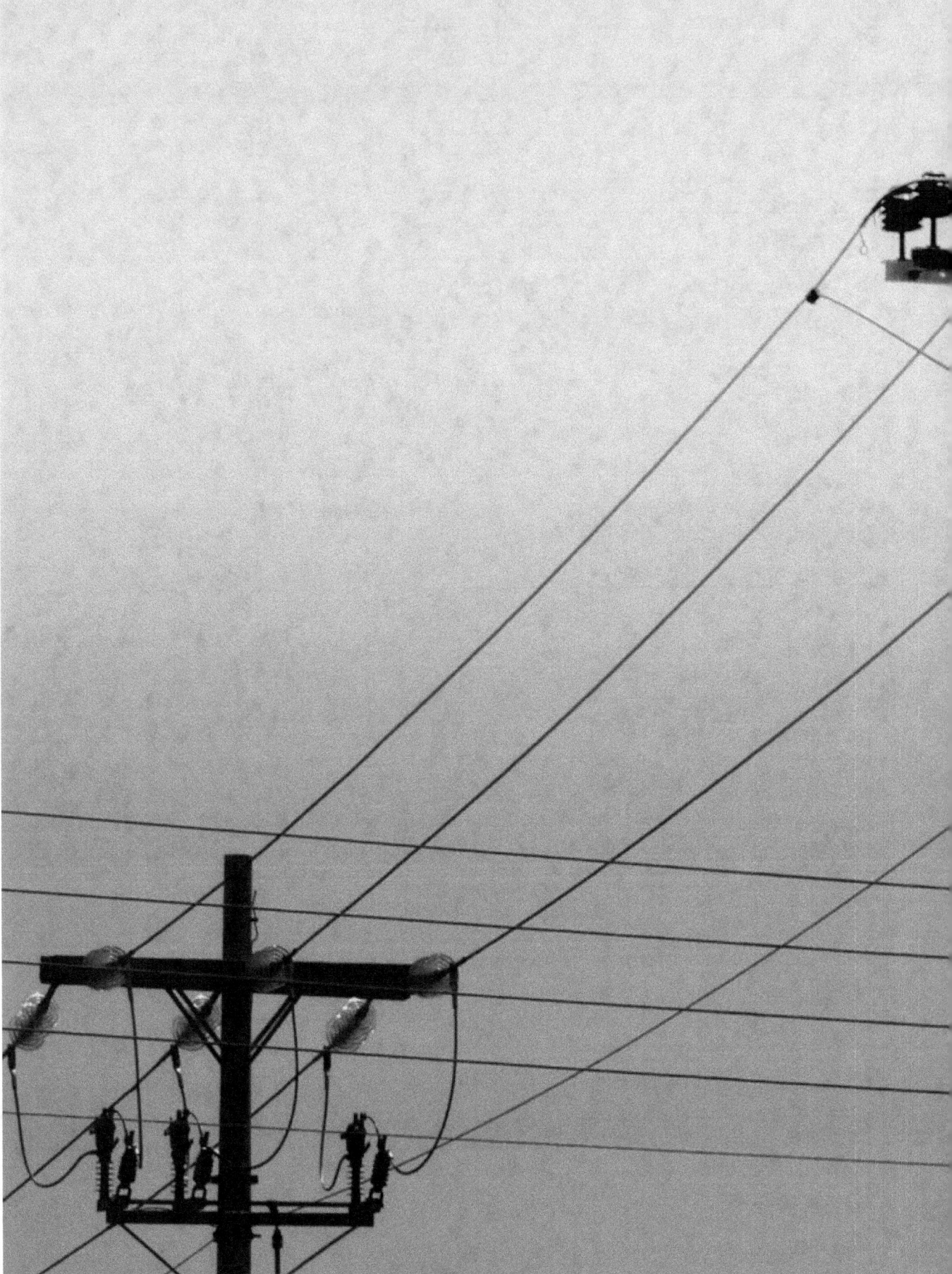

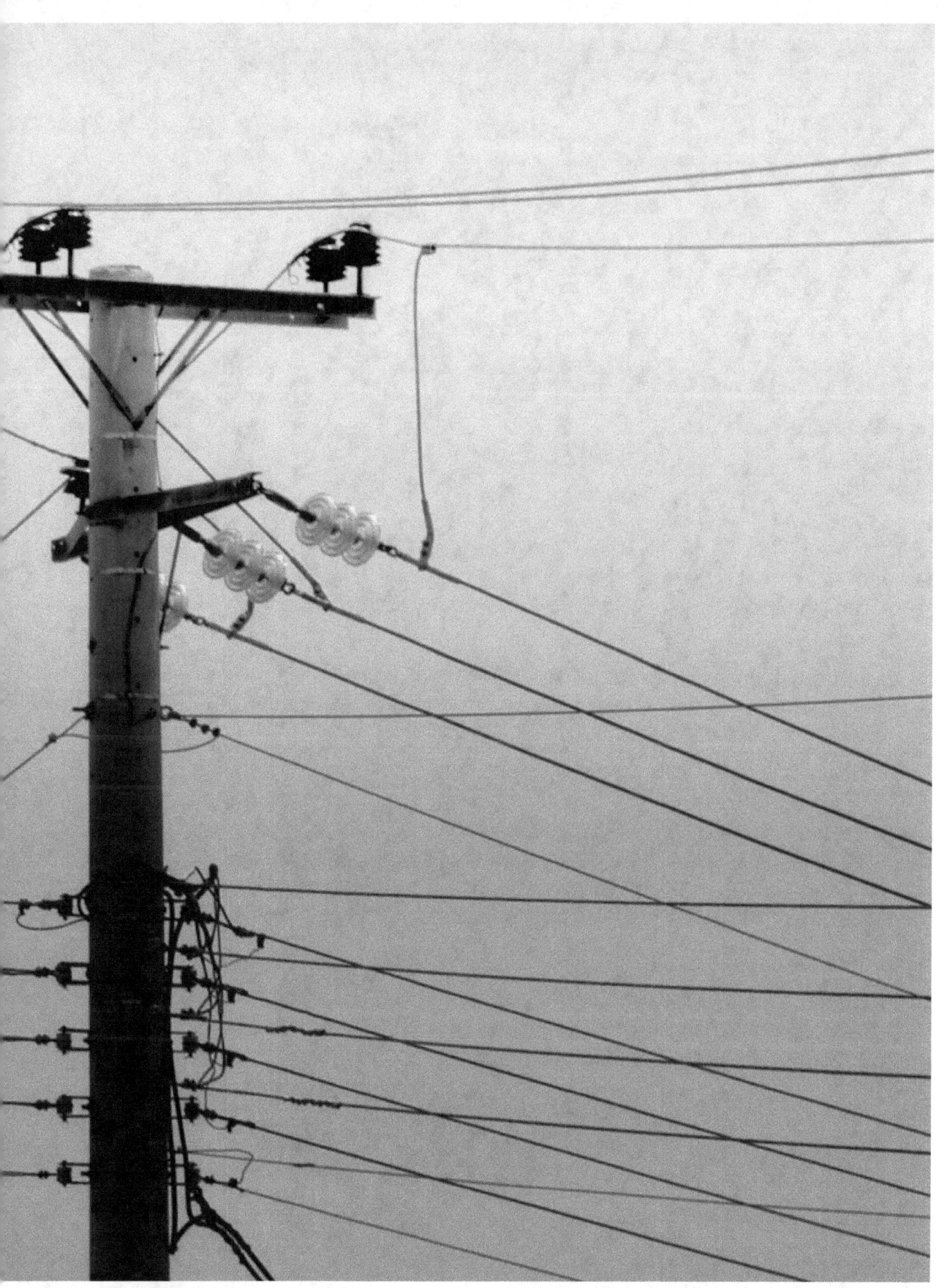

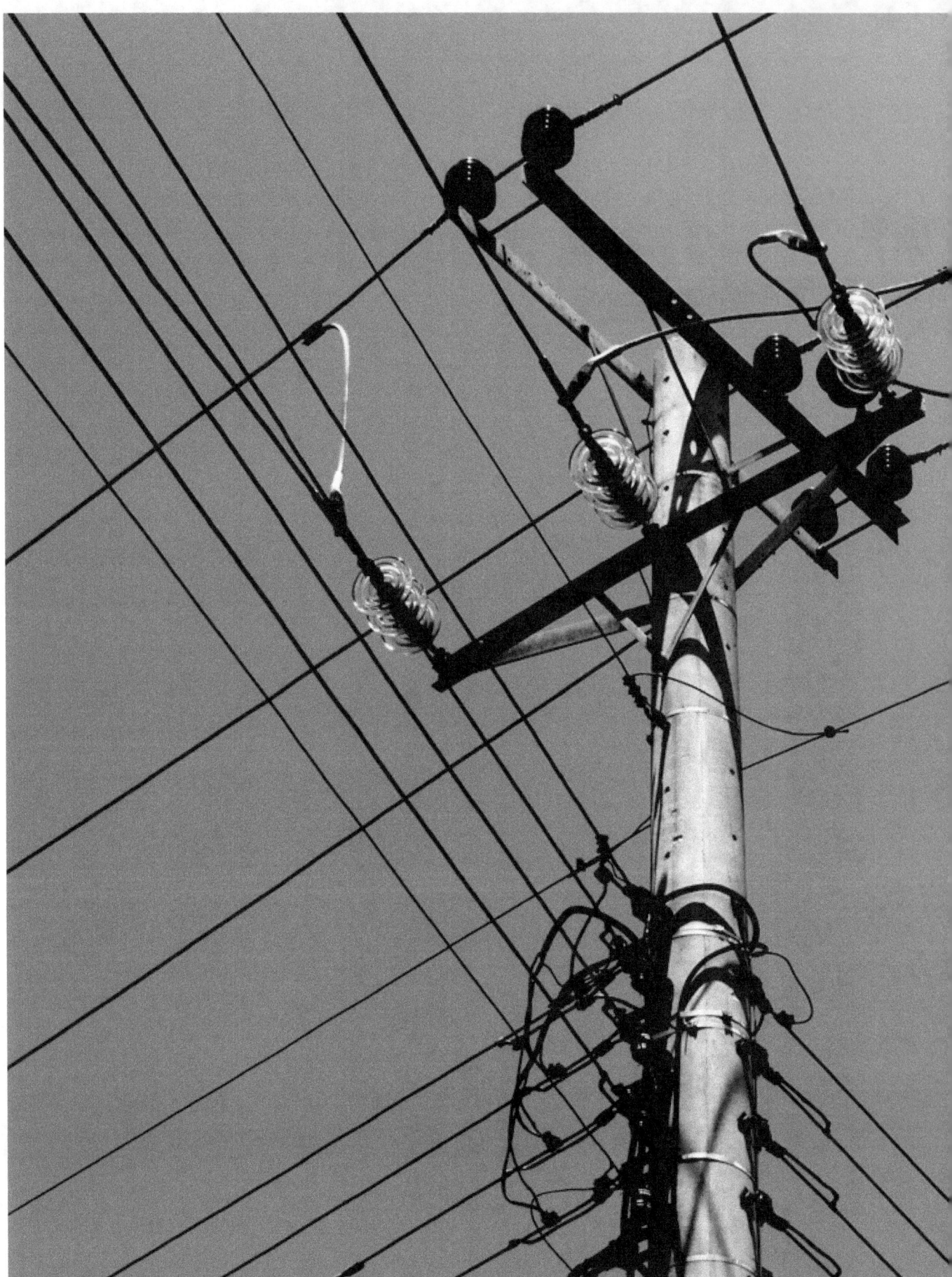

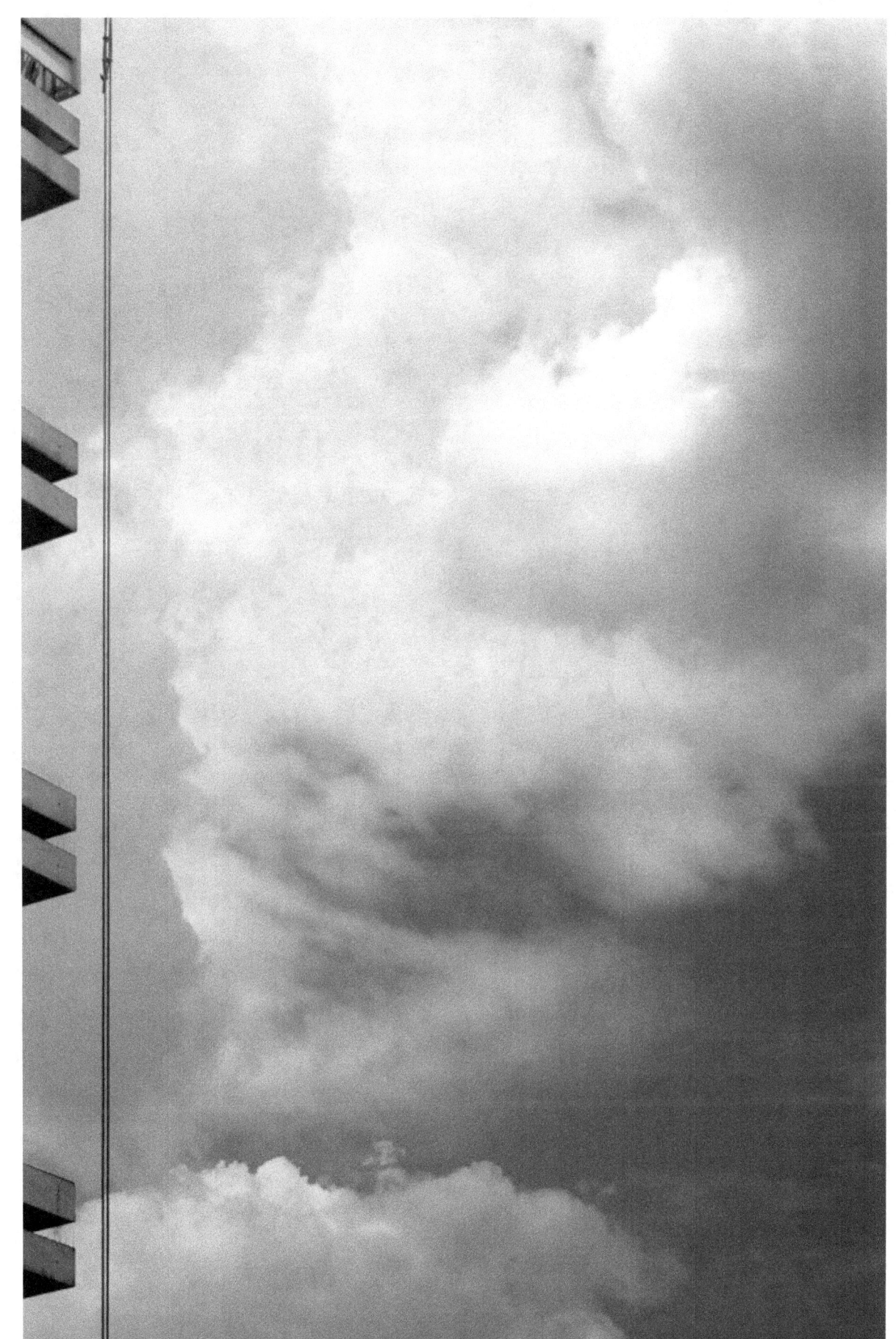

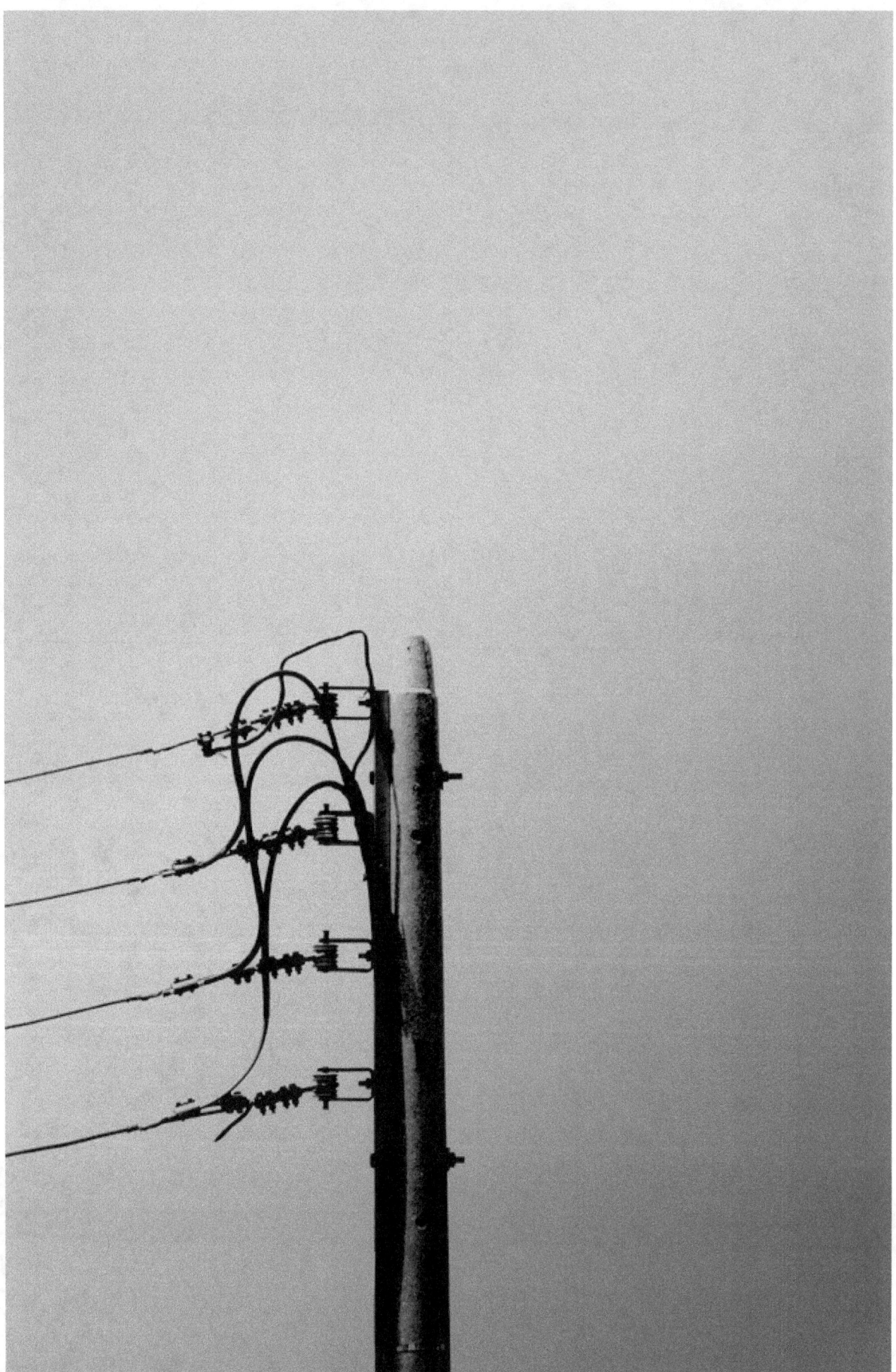

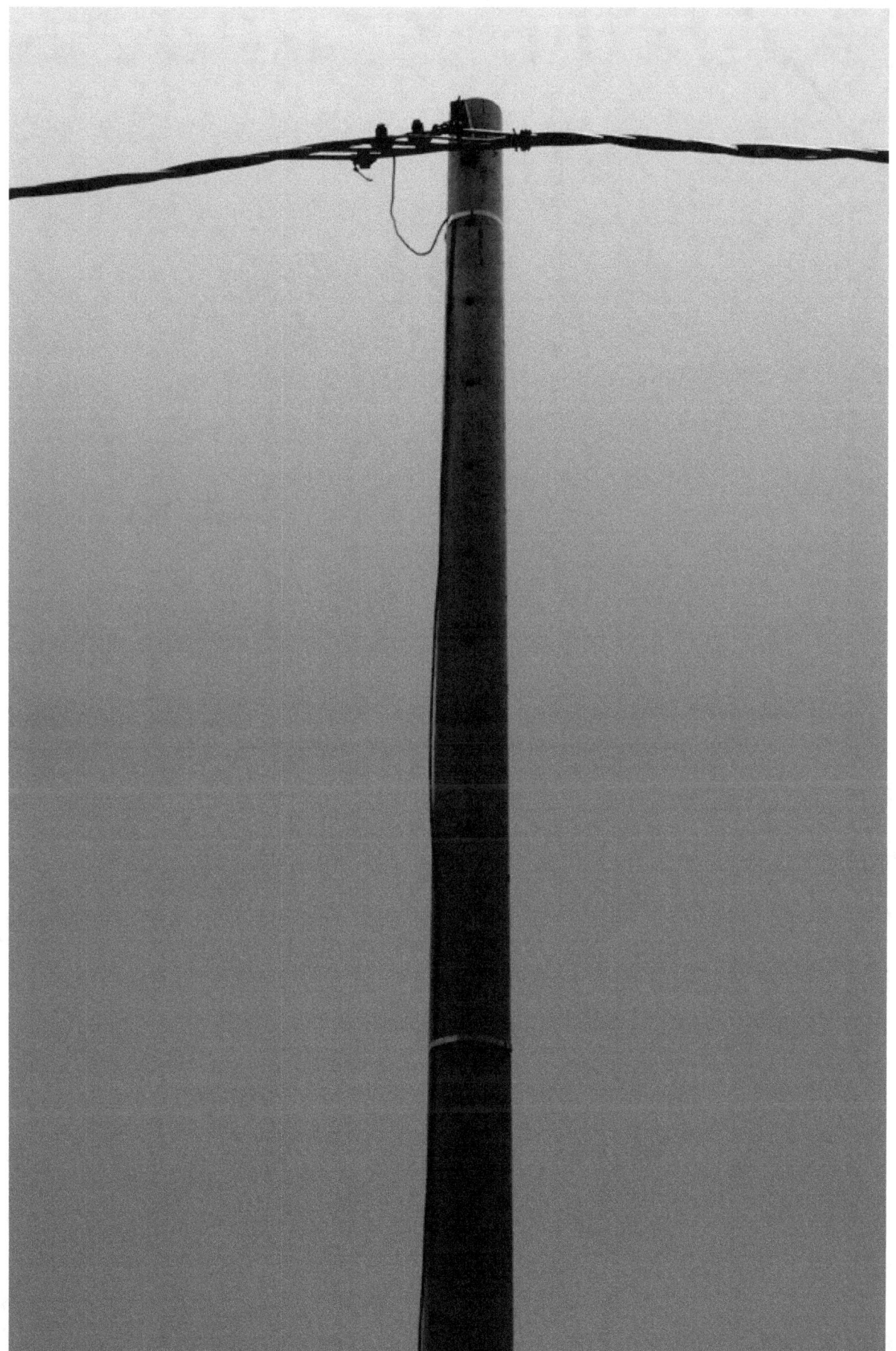

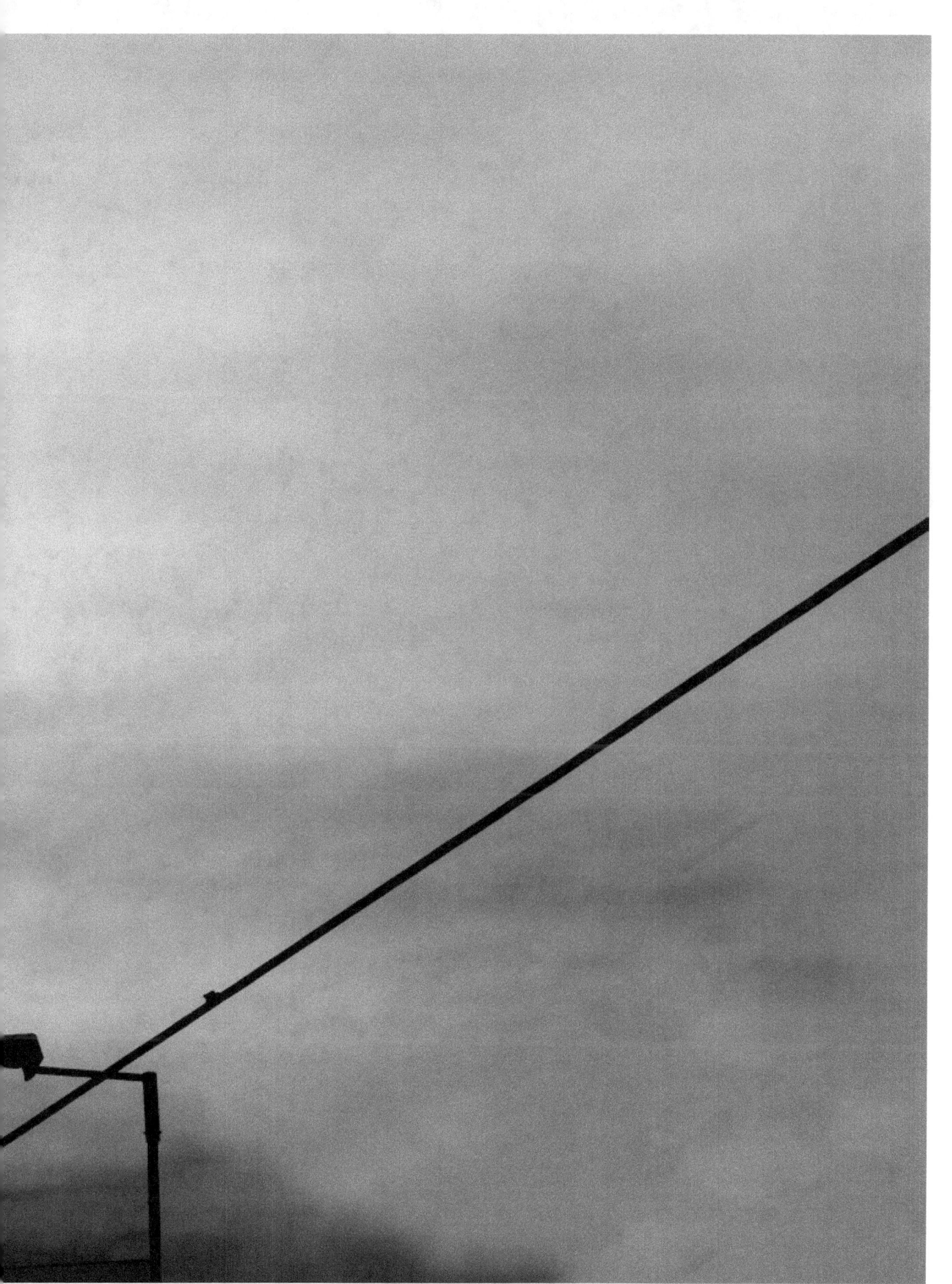

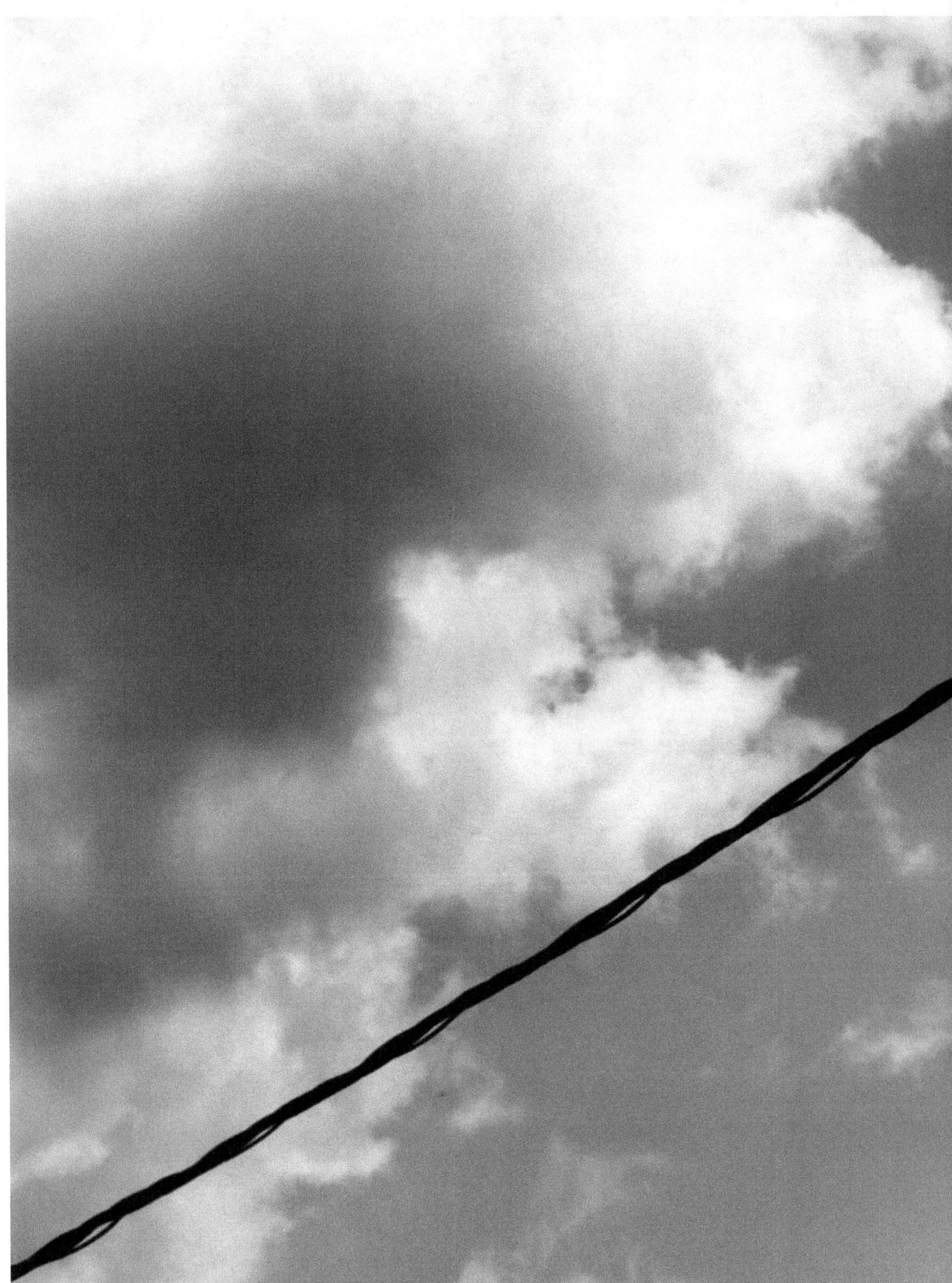

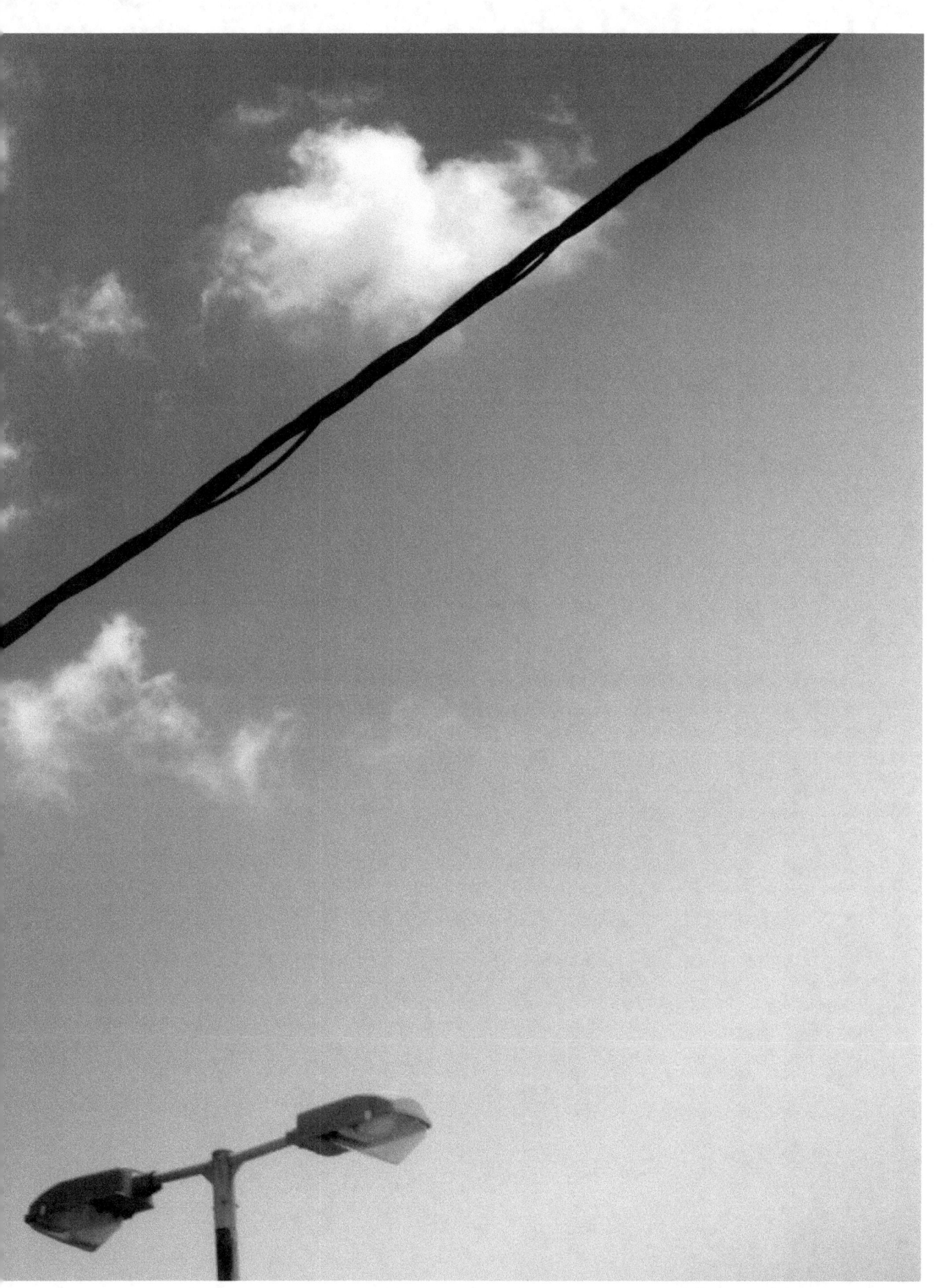

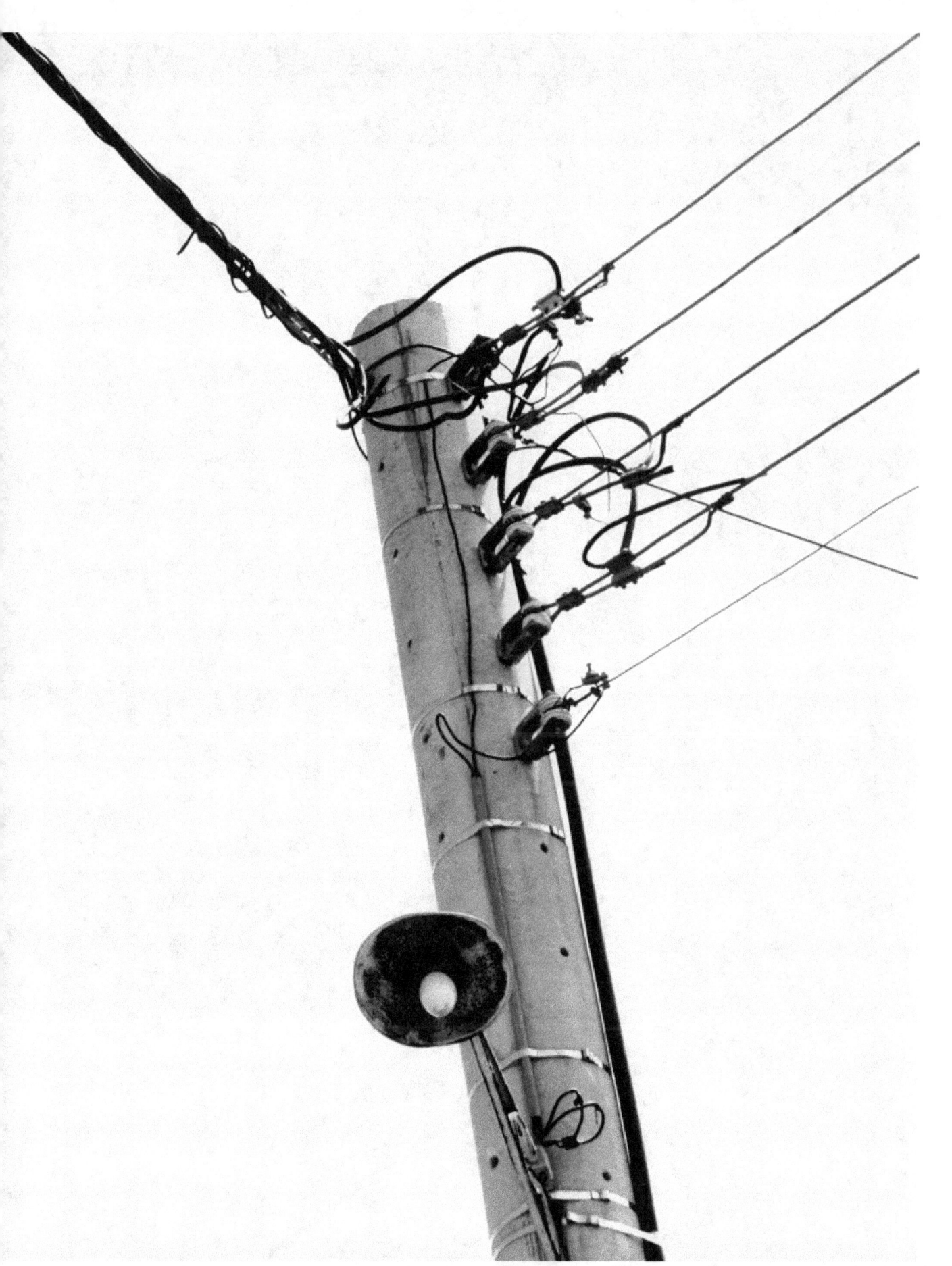

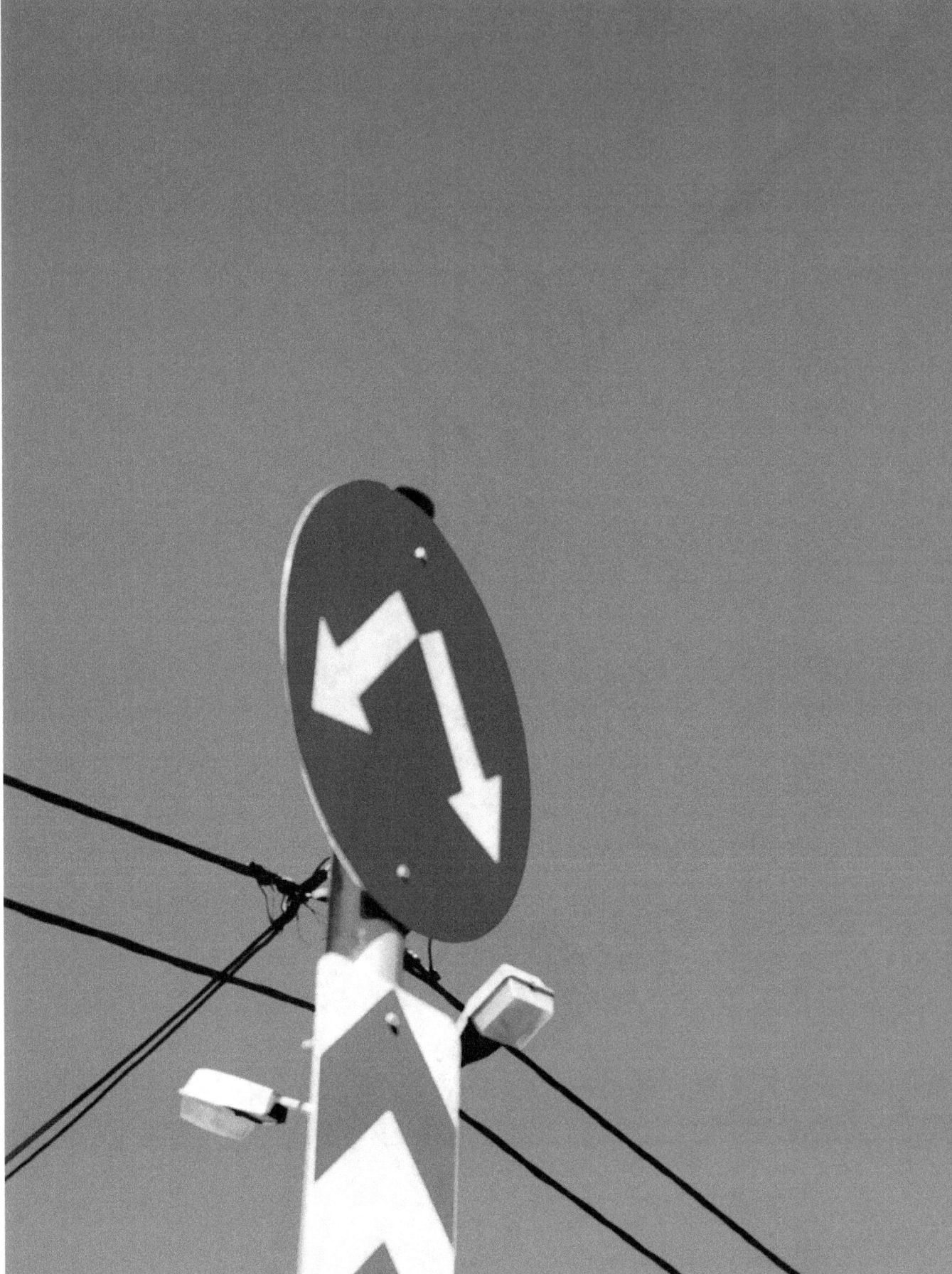

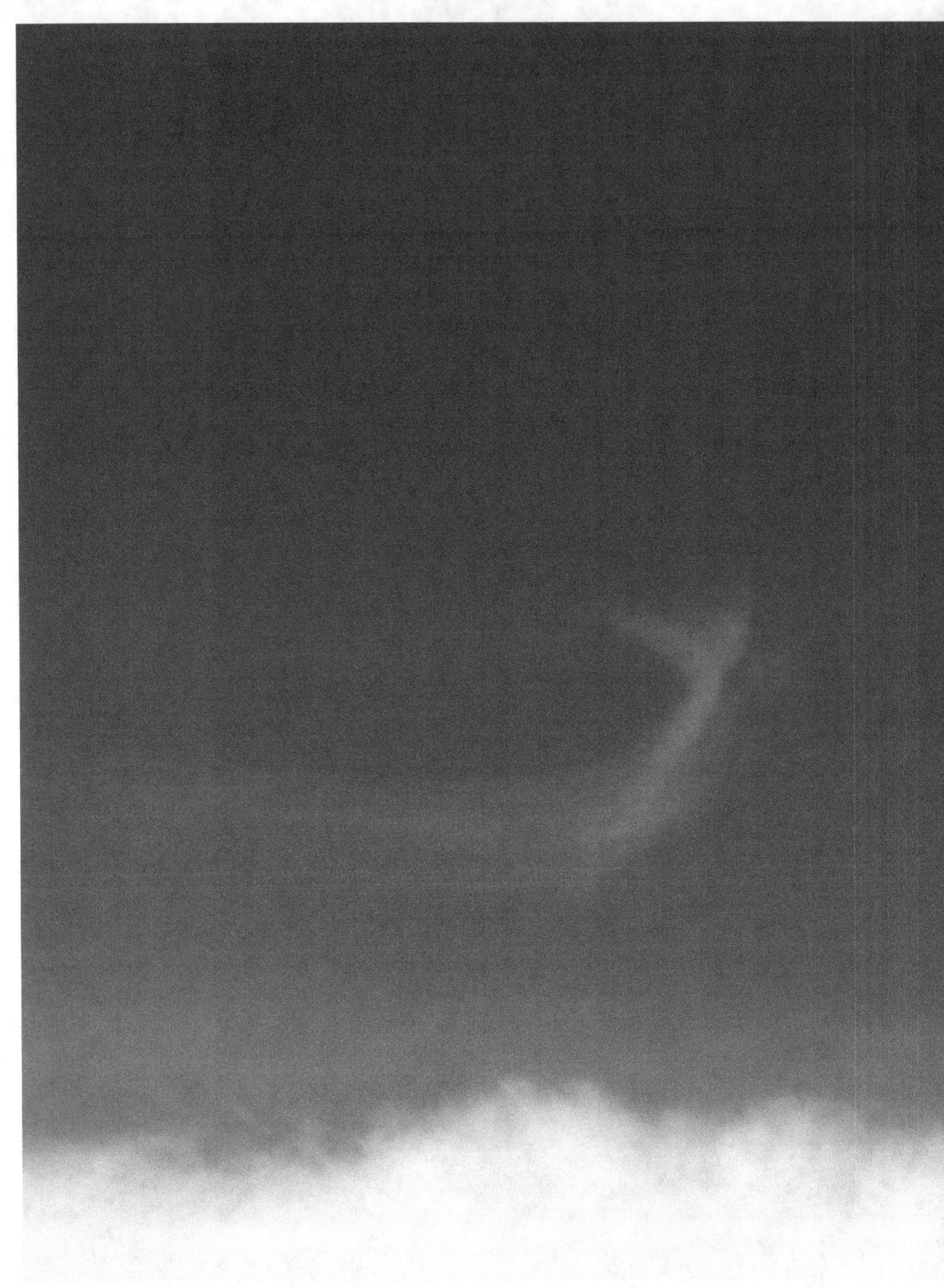

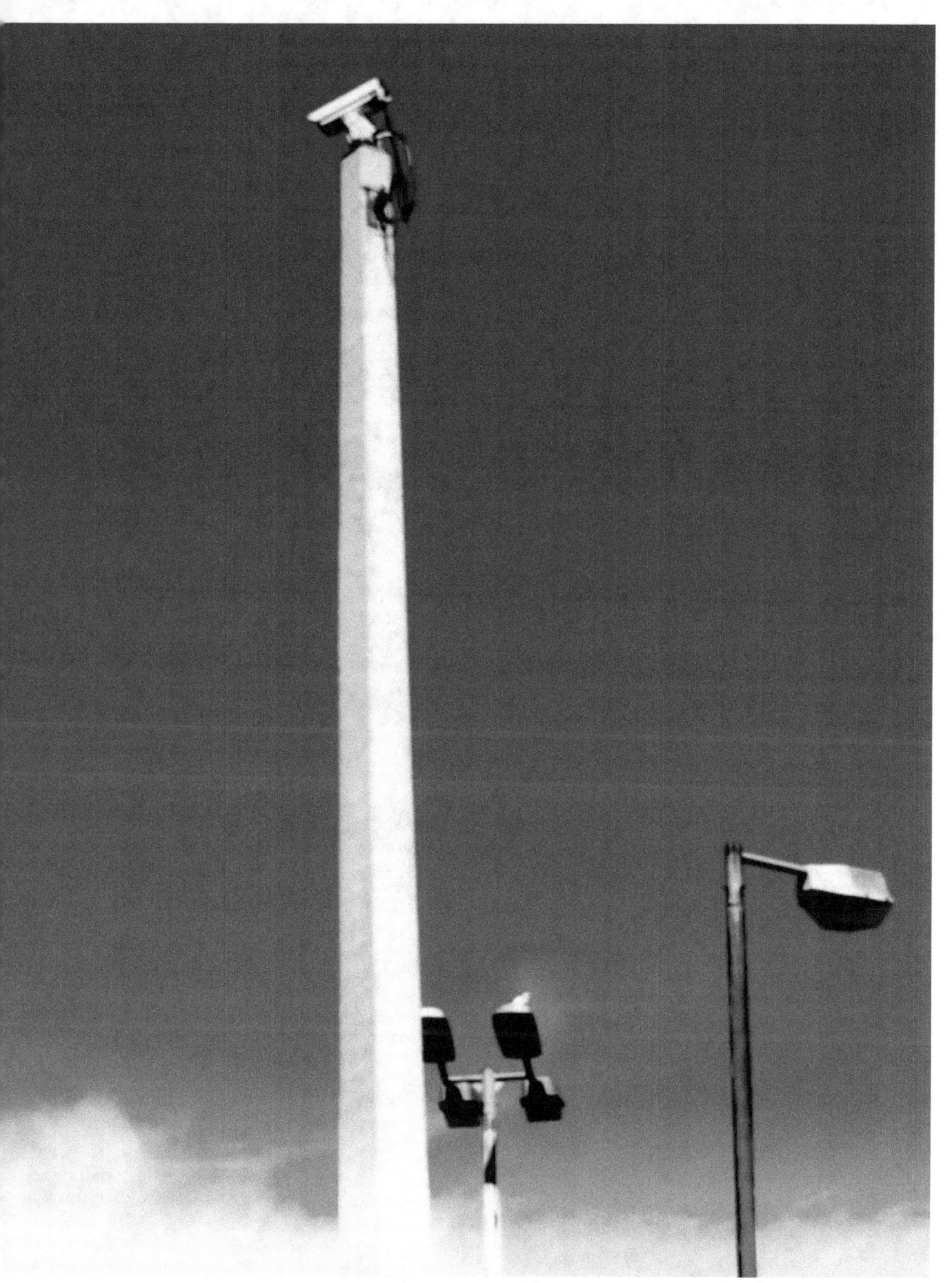

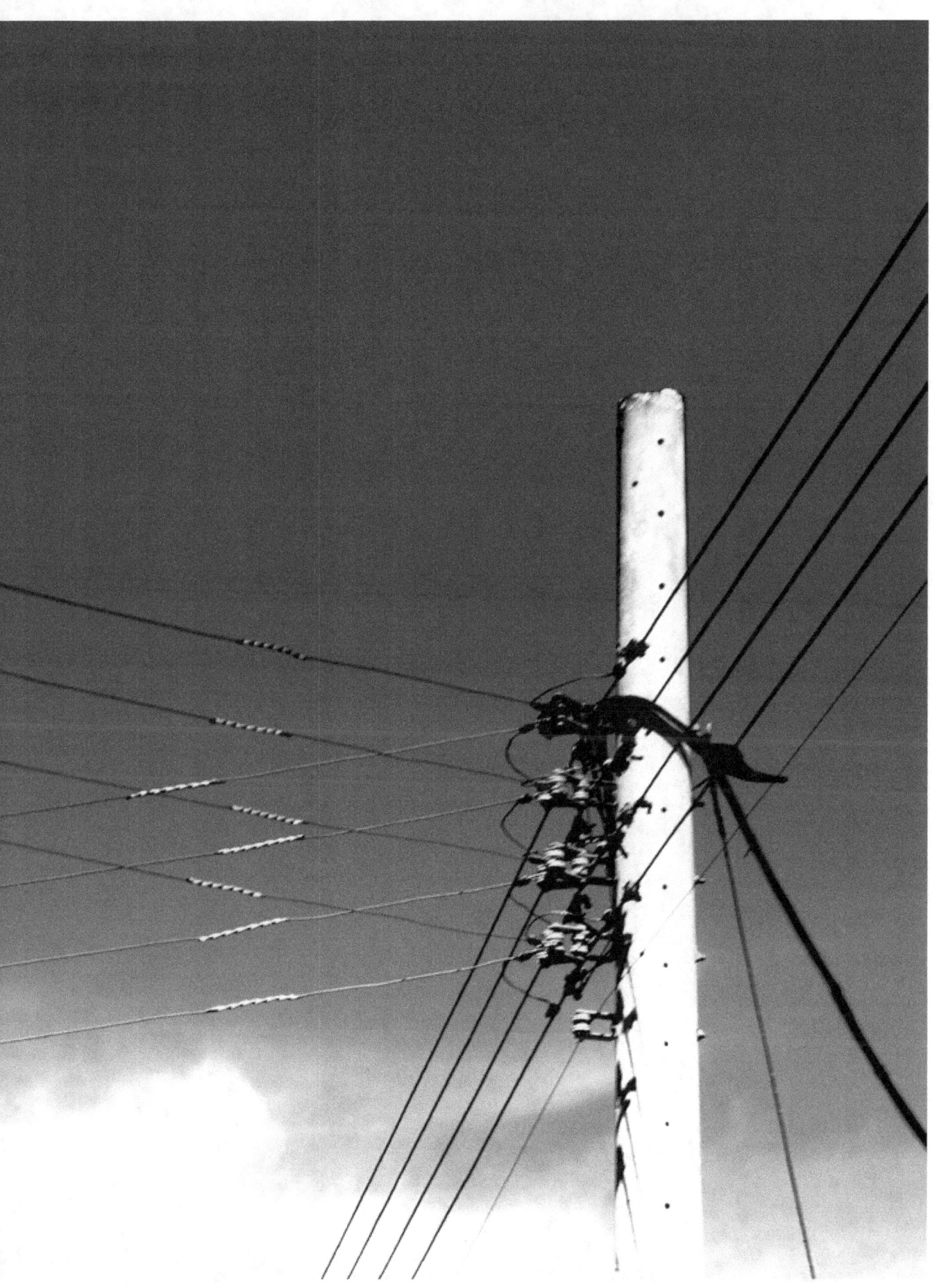

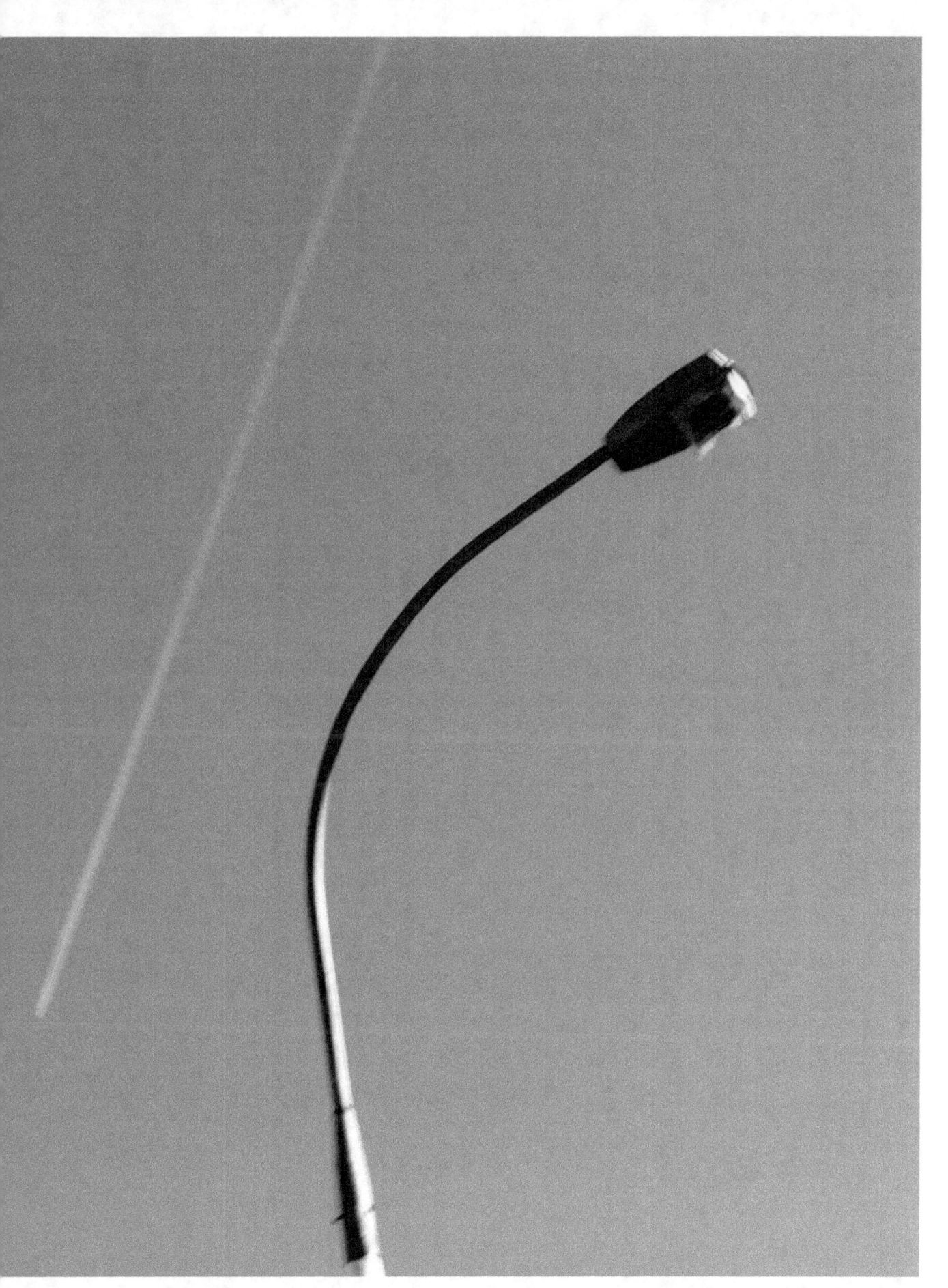

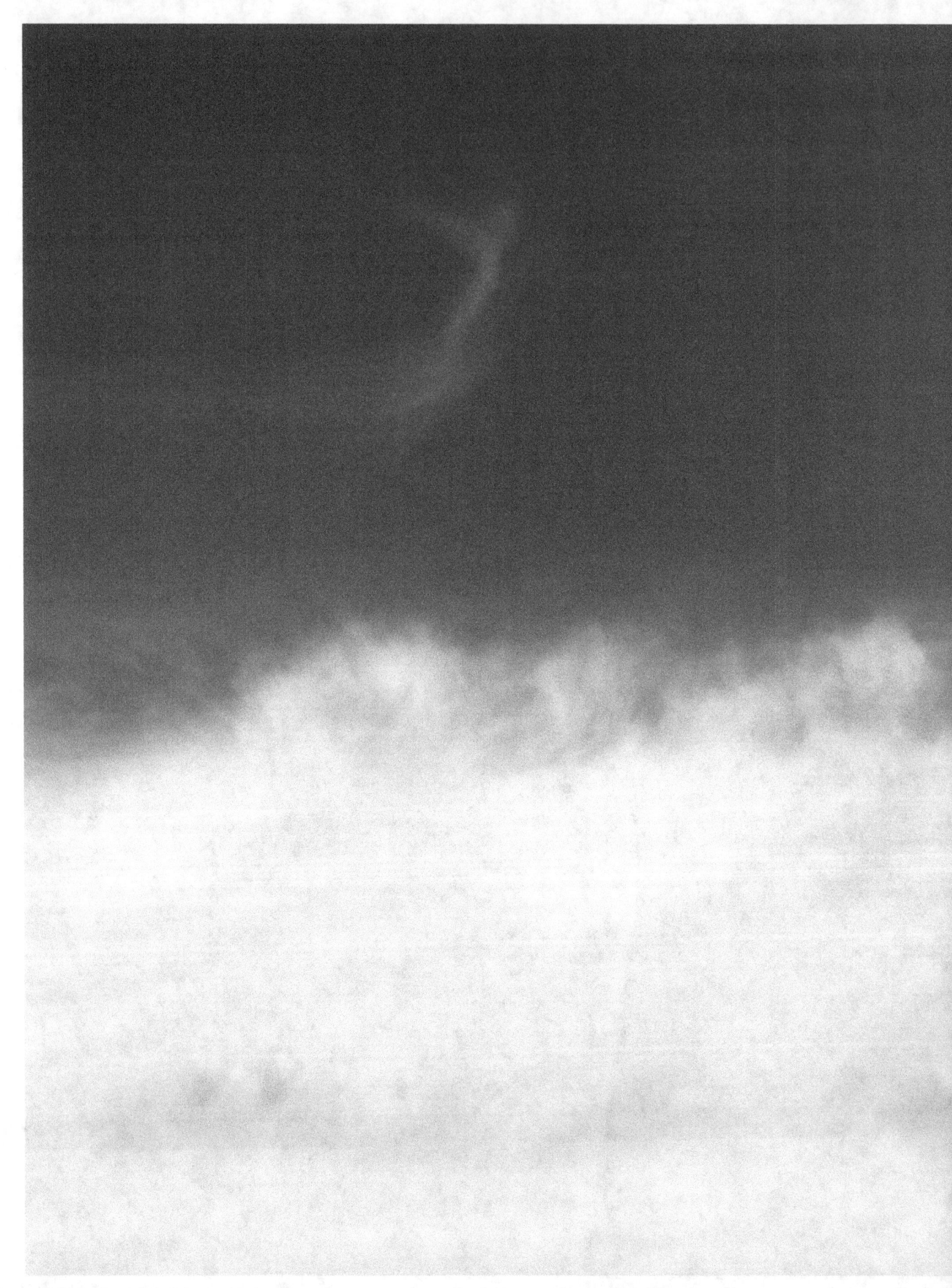

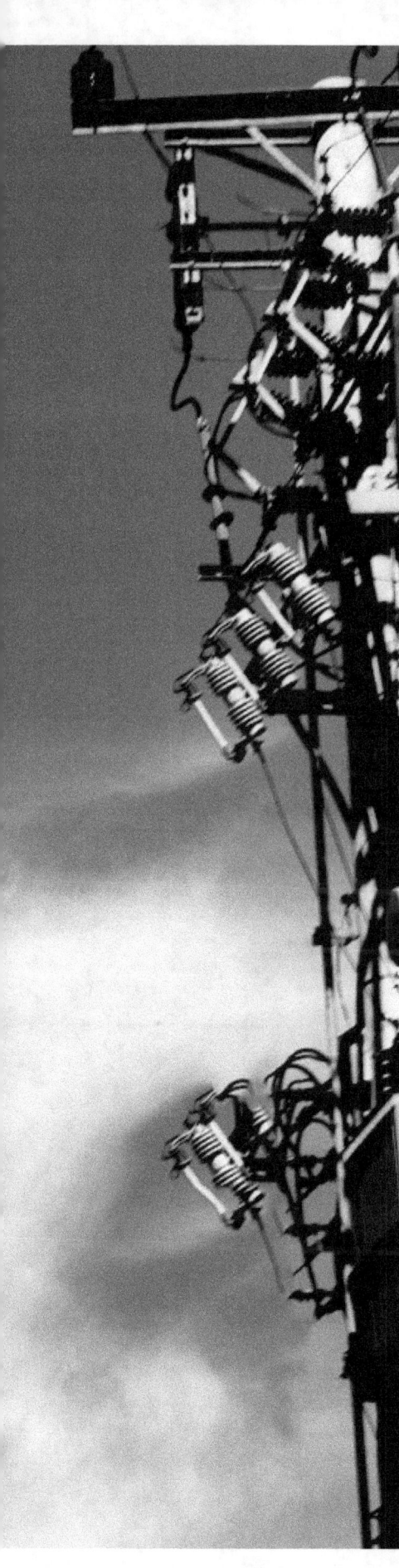

Urban
Summits

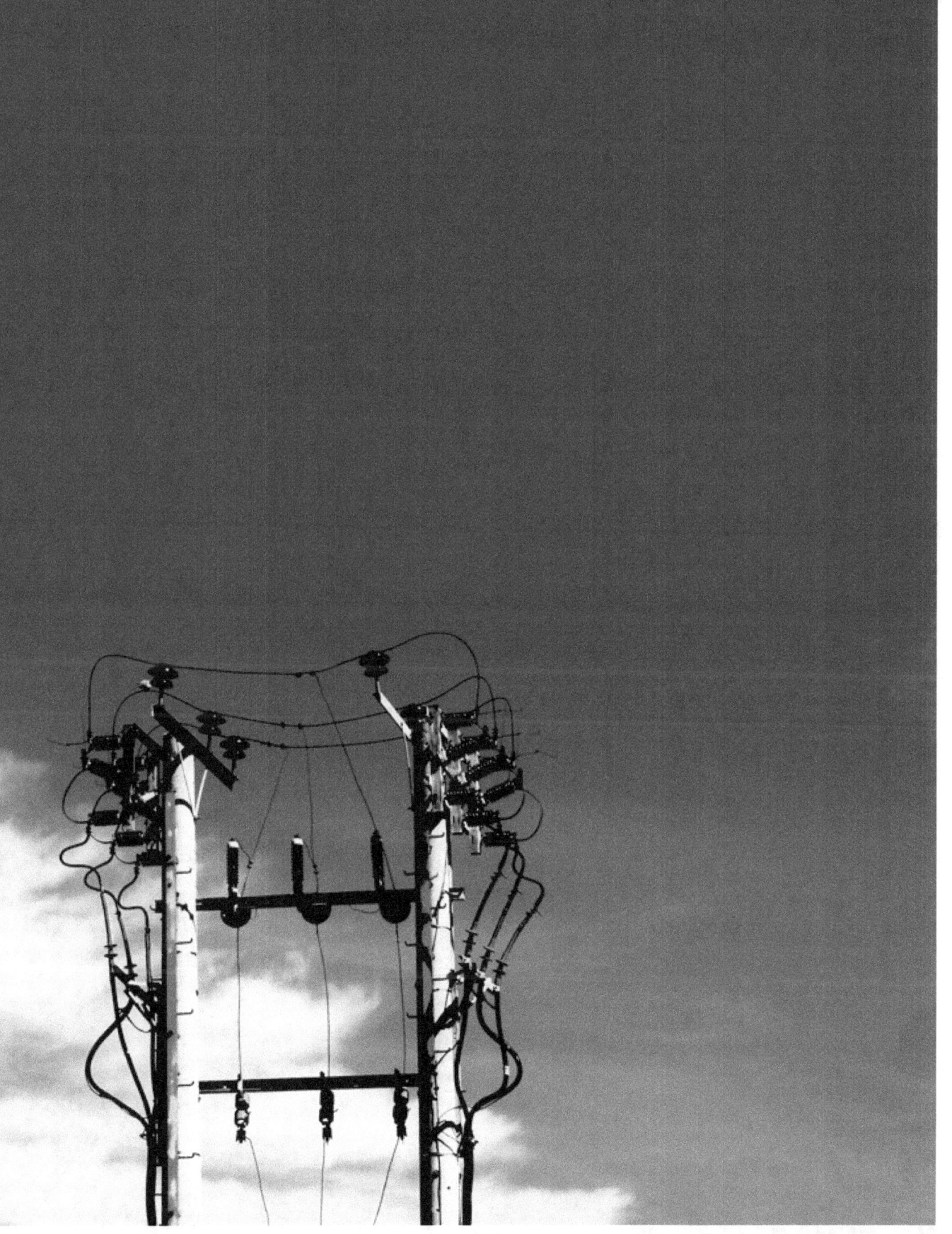

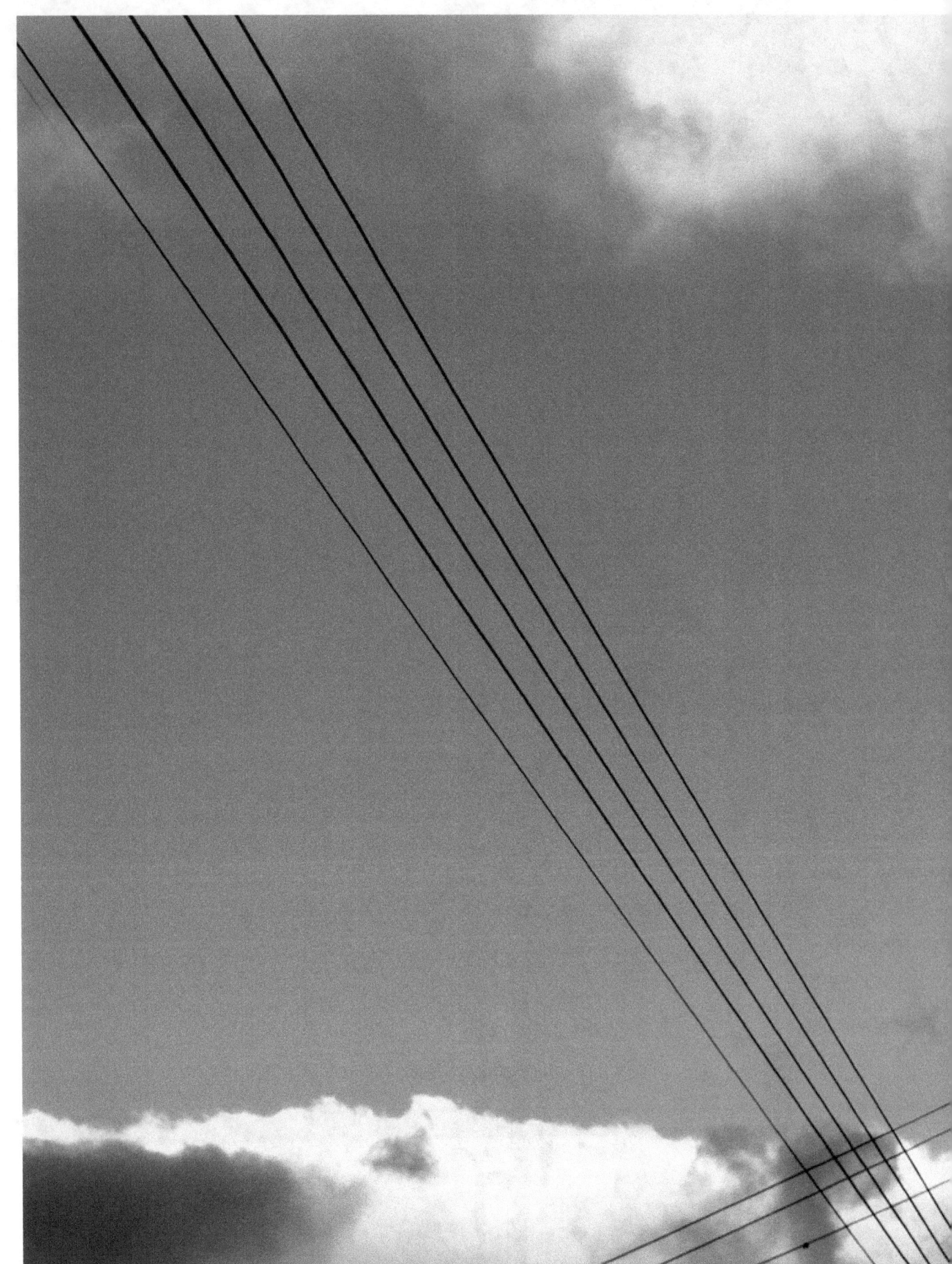

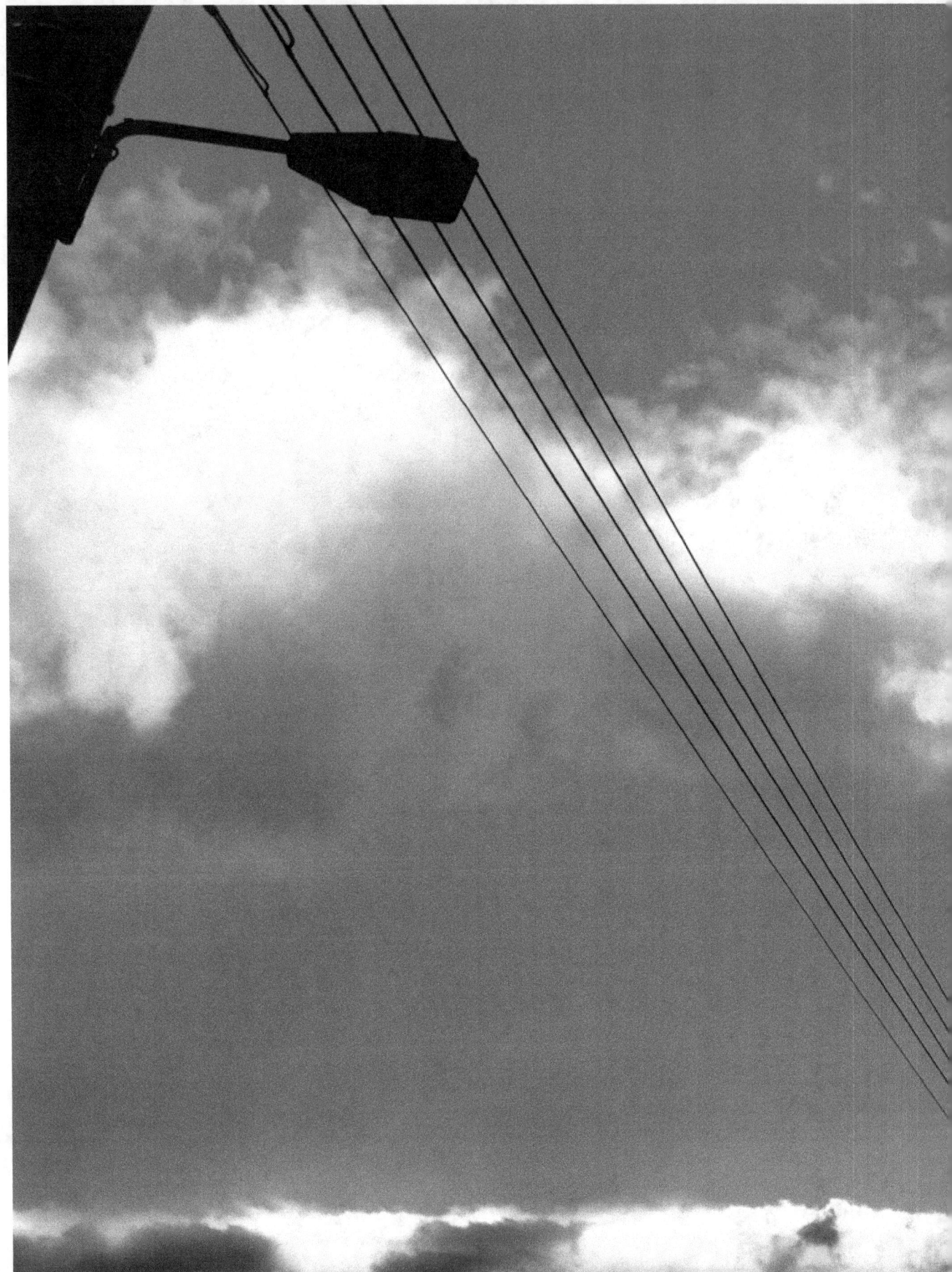

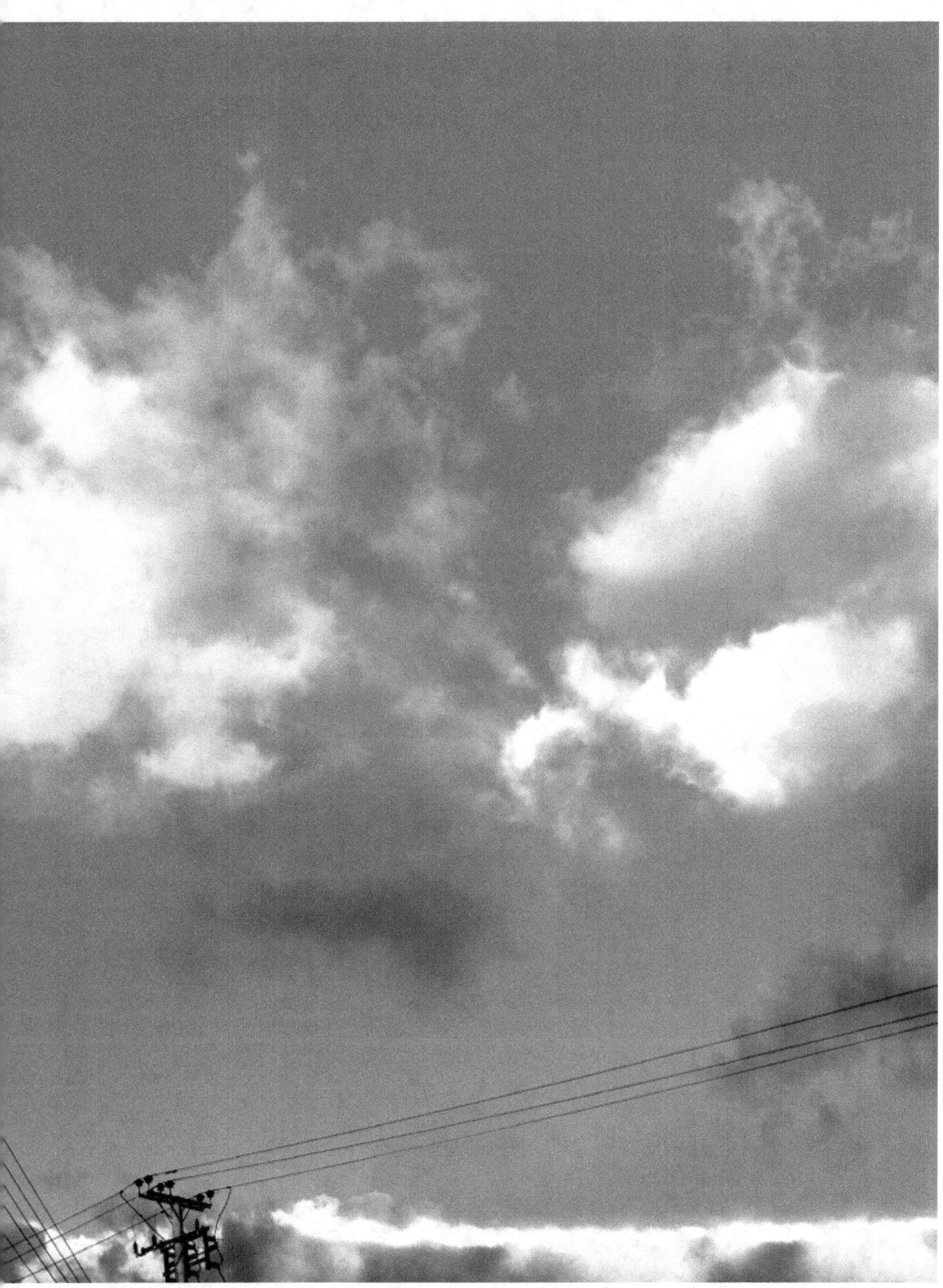

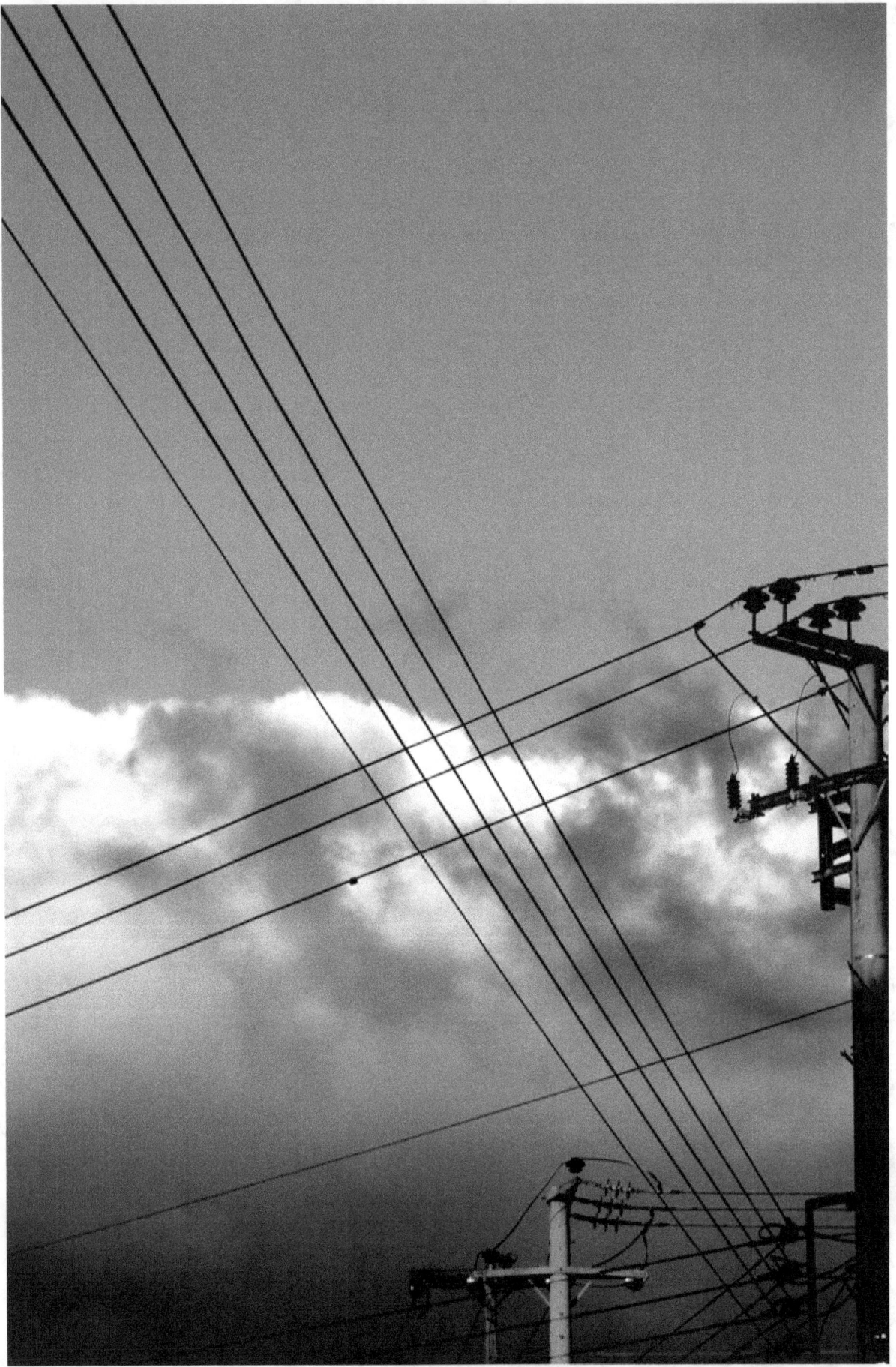

occupying
earth and sky

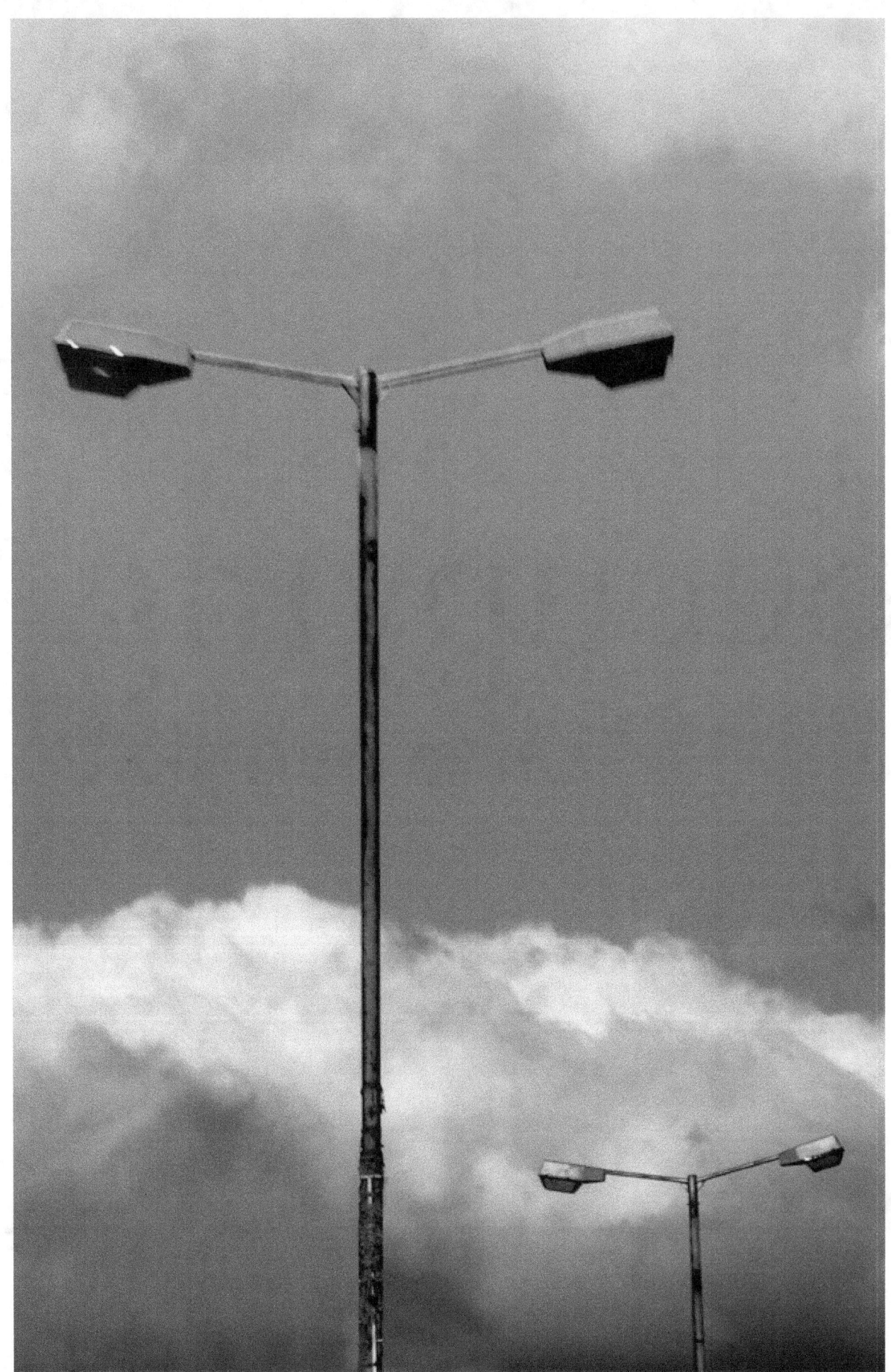

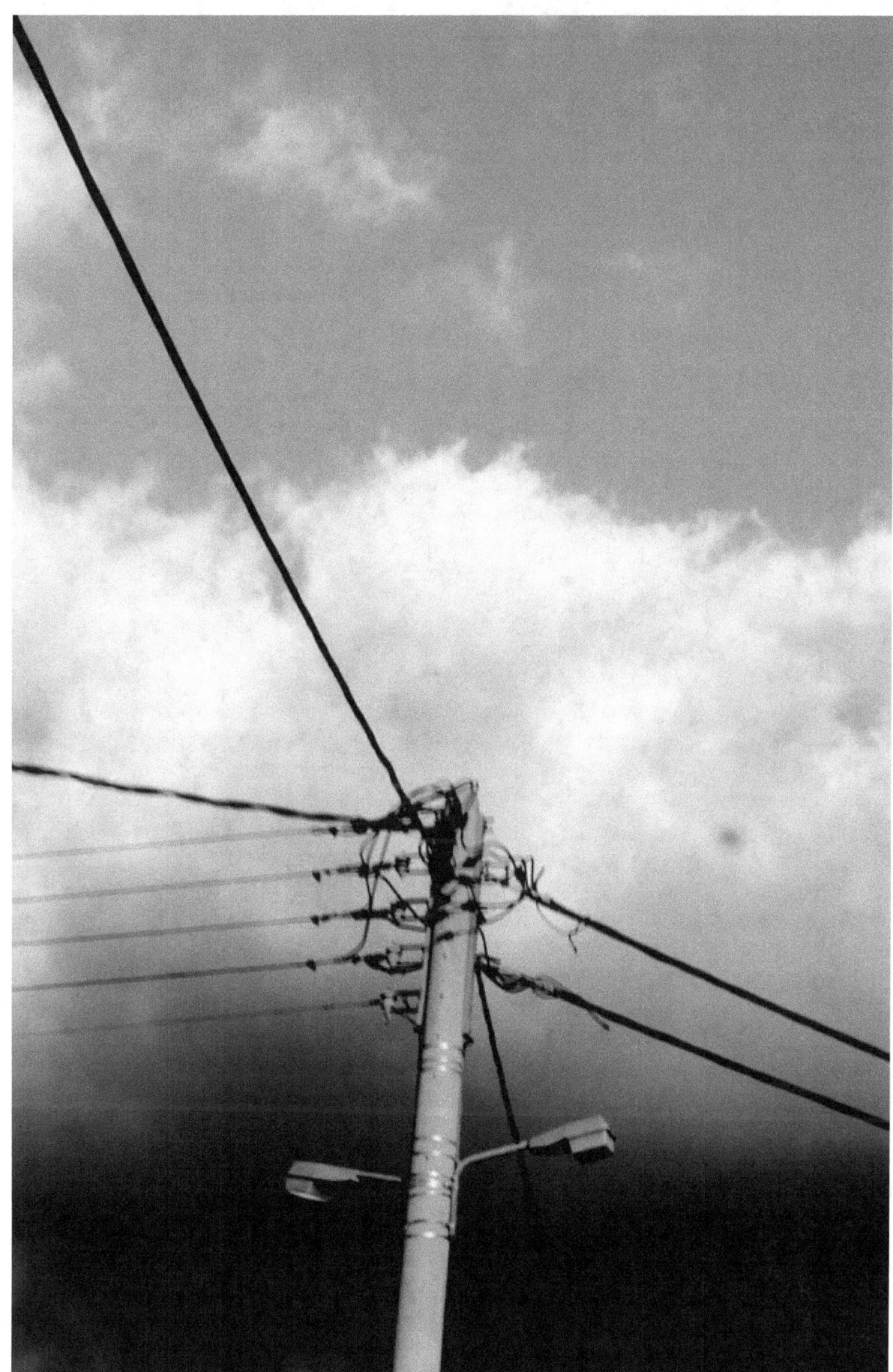

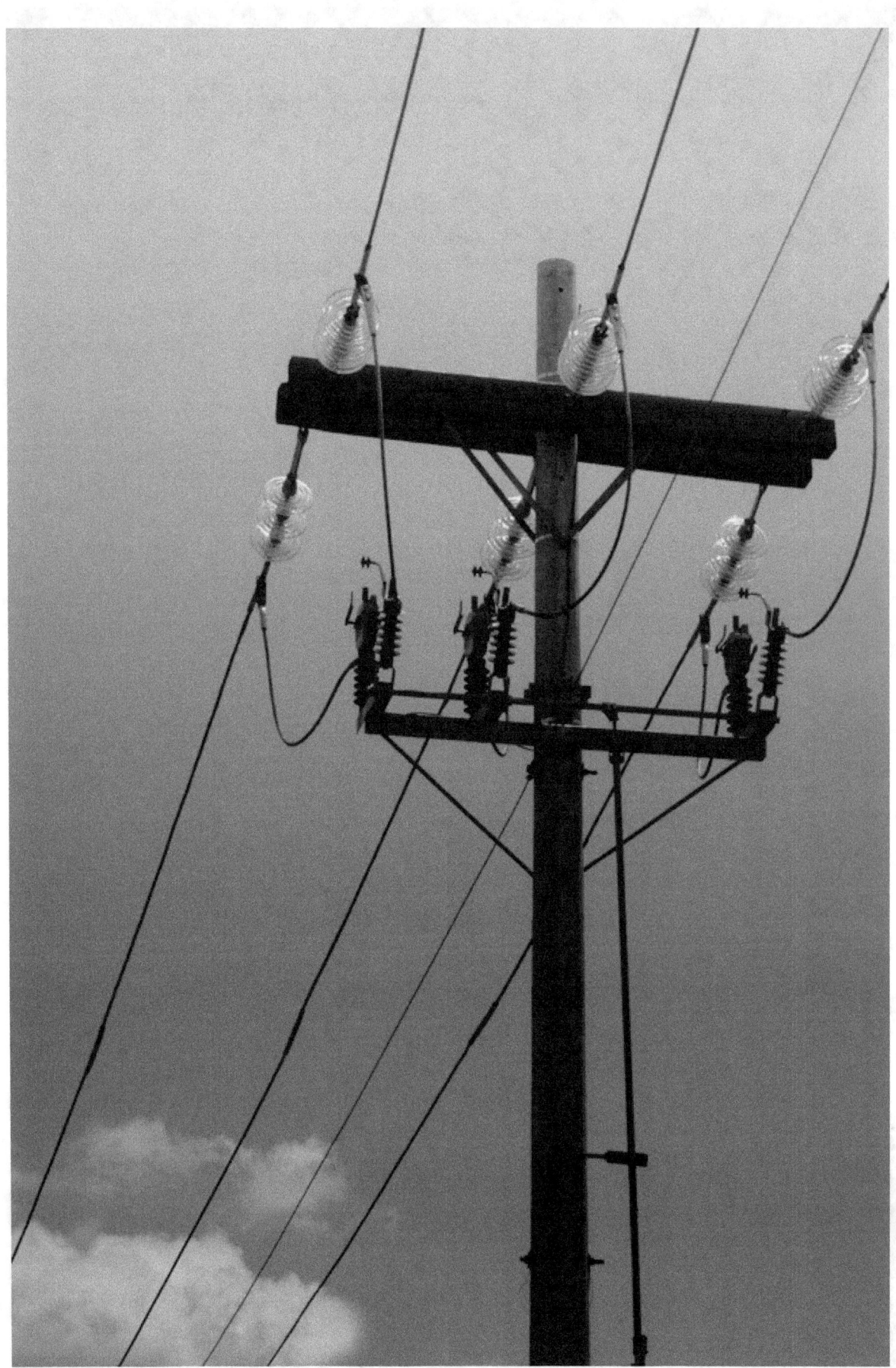

From one point
to another
waves of white
I am an artist
I paint the ground
with shadows
& lights.

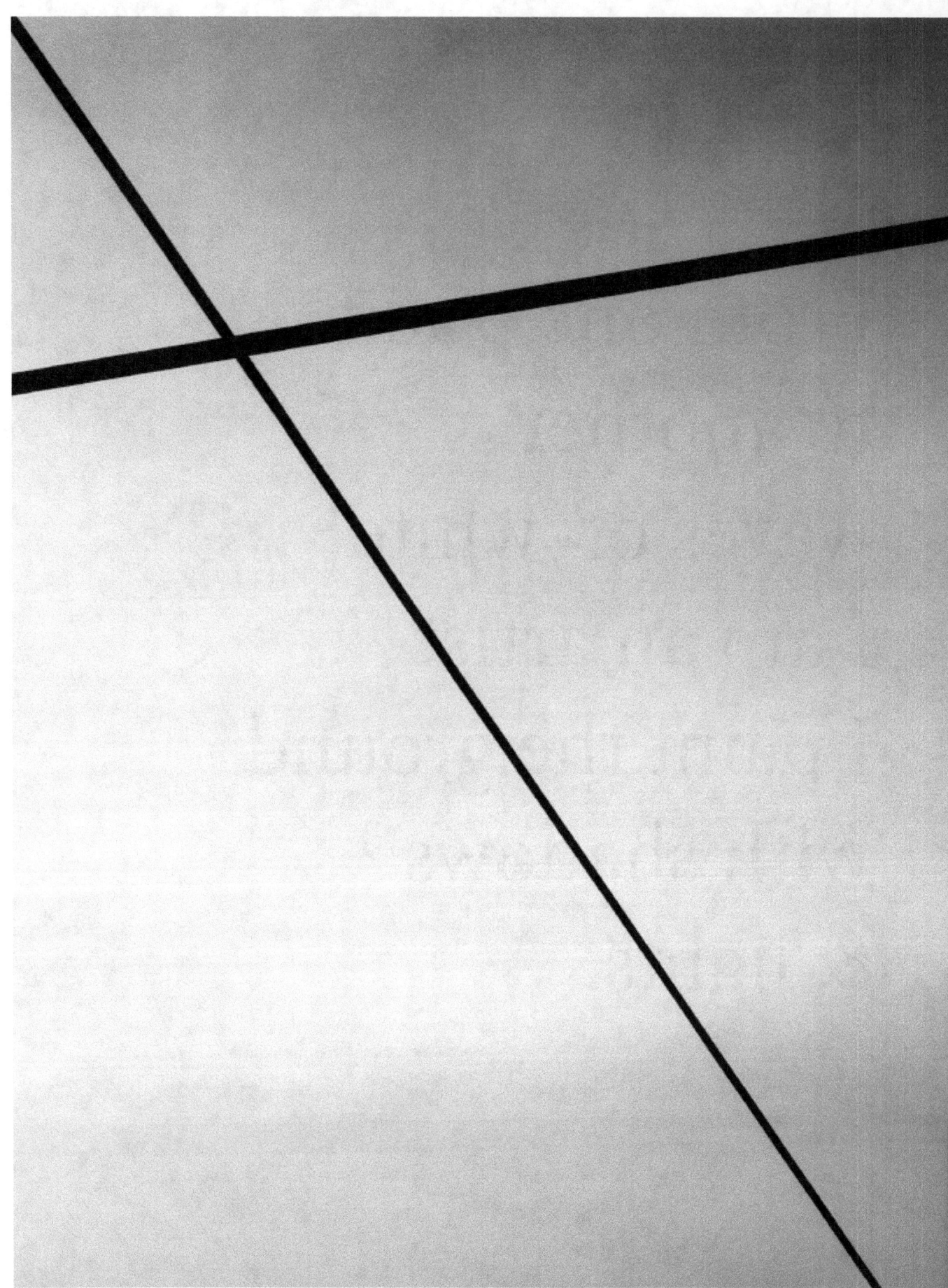

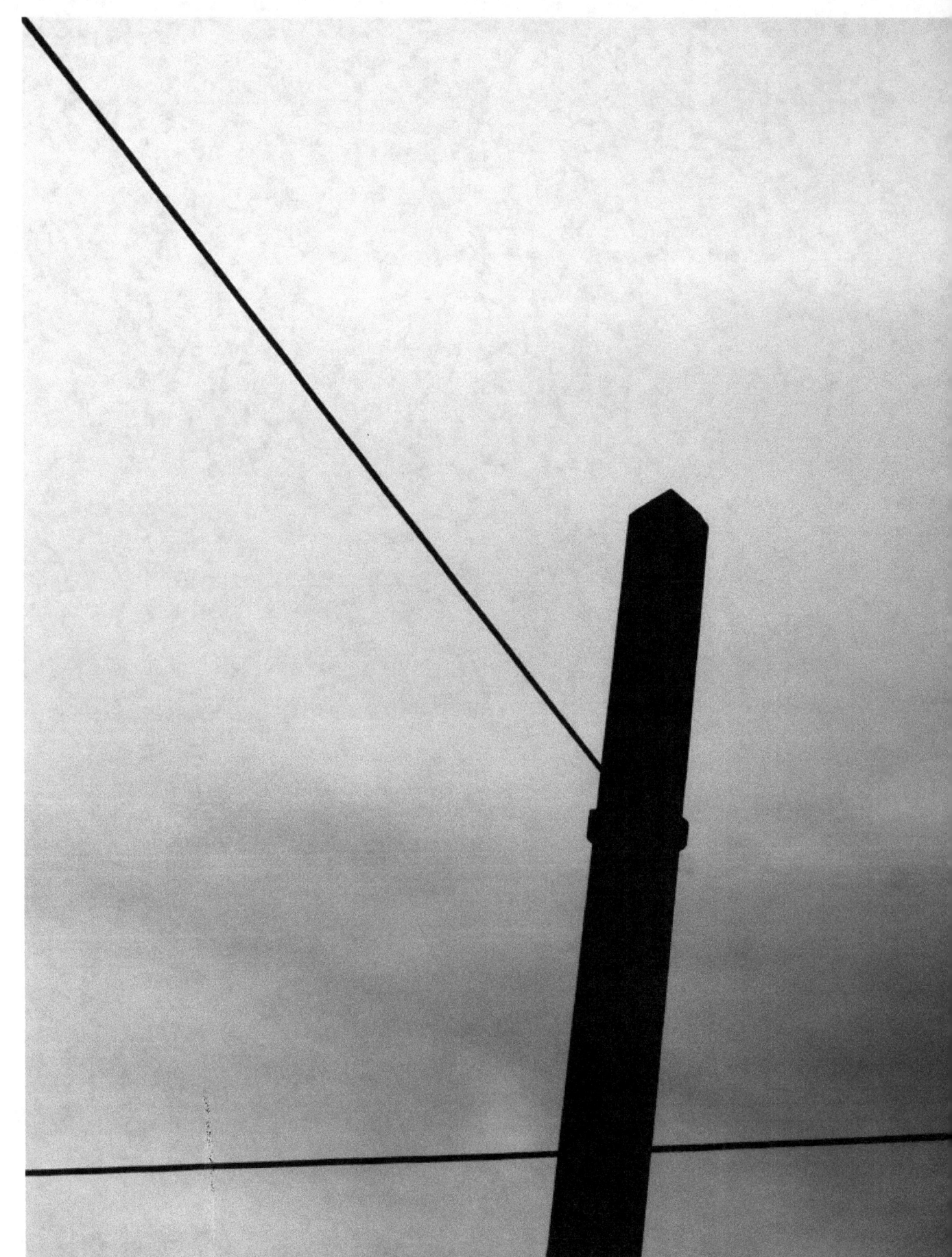

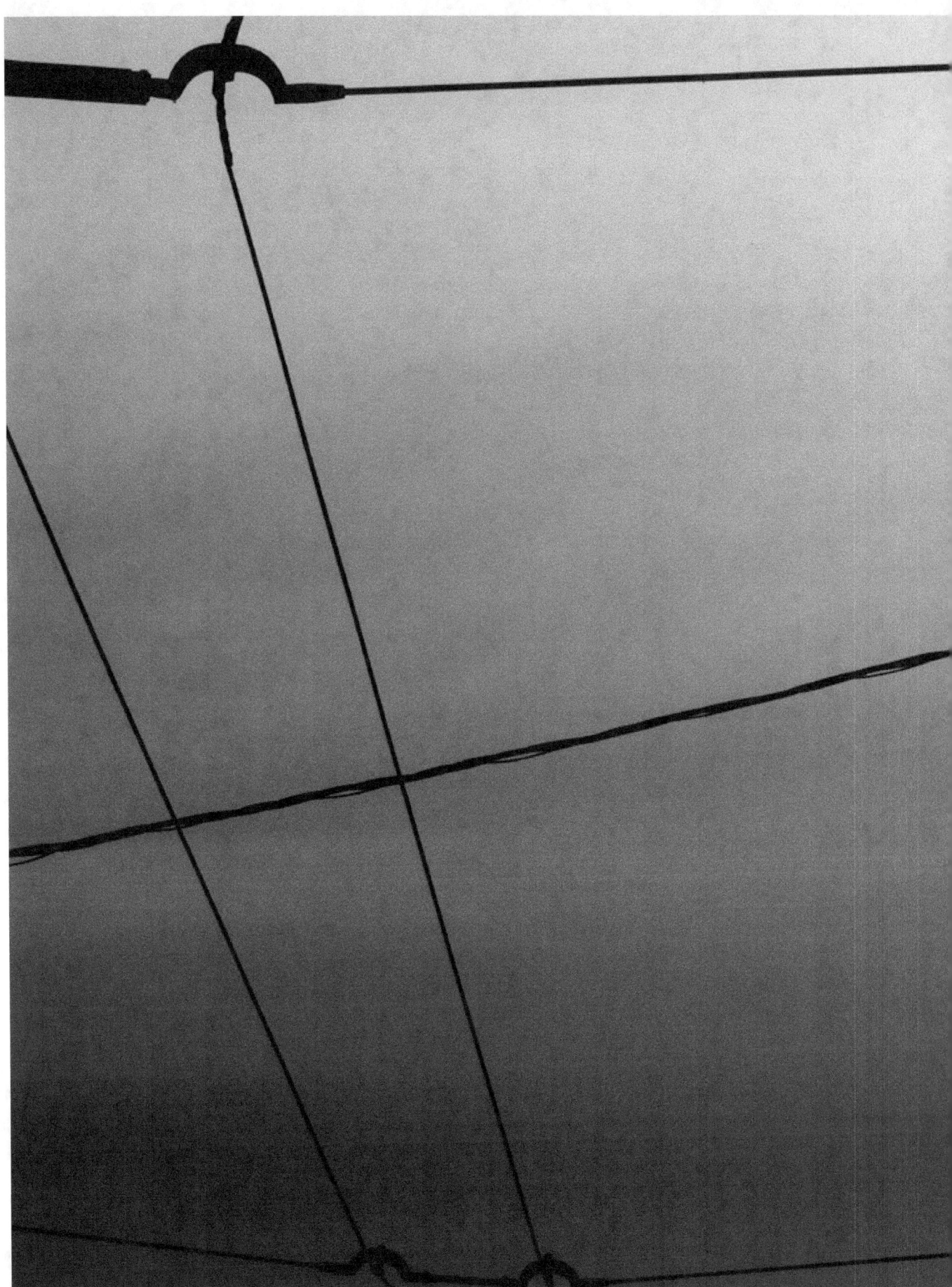

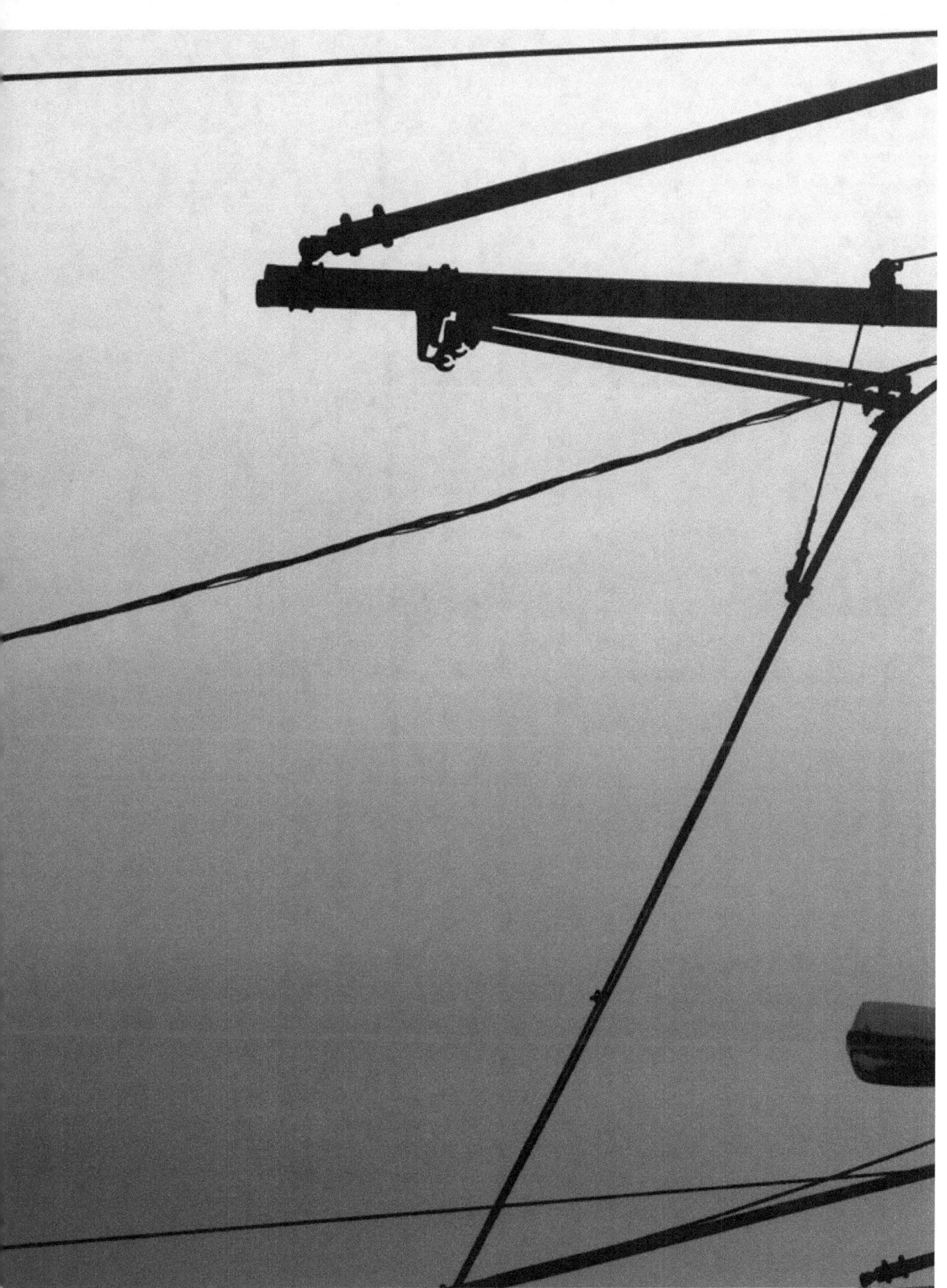

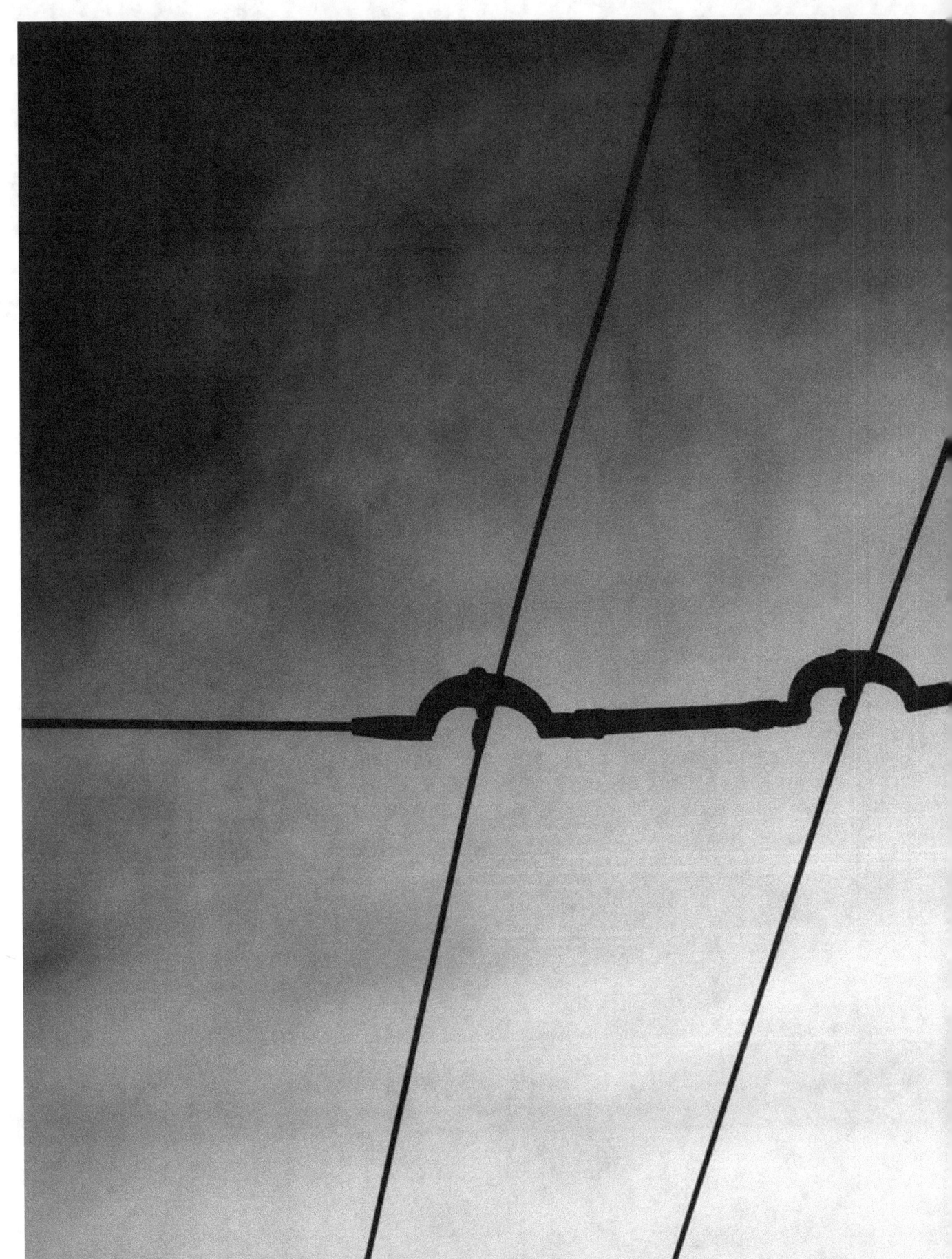

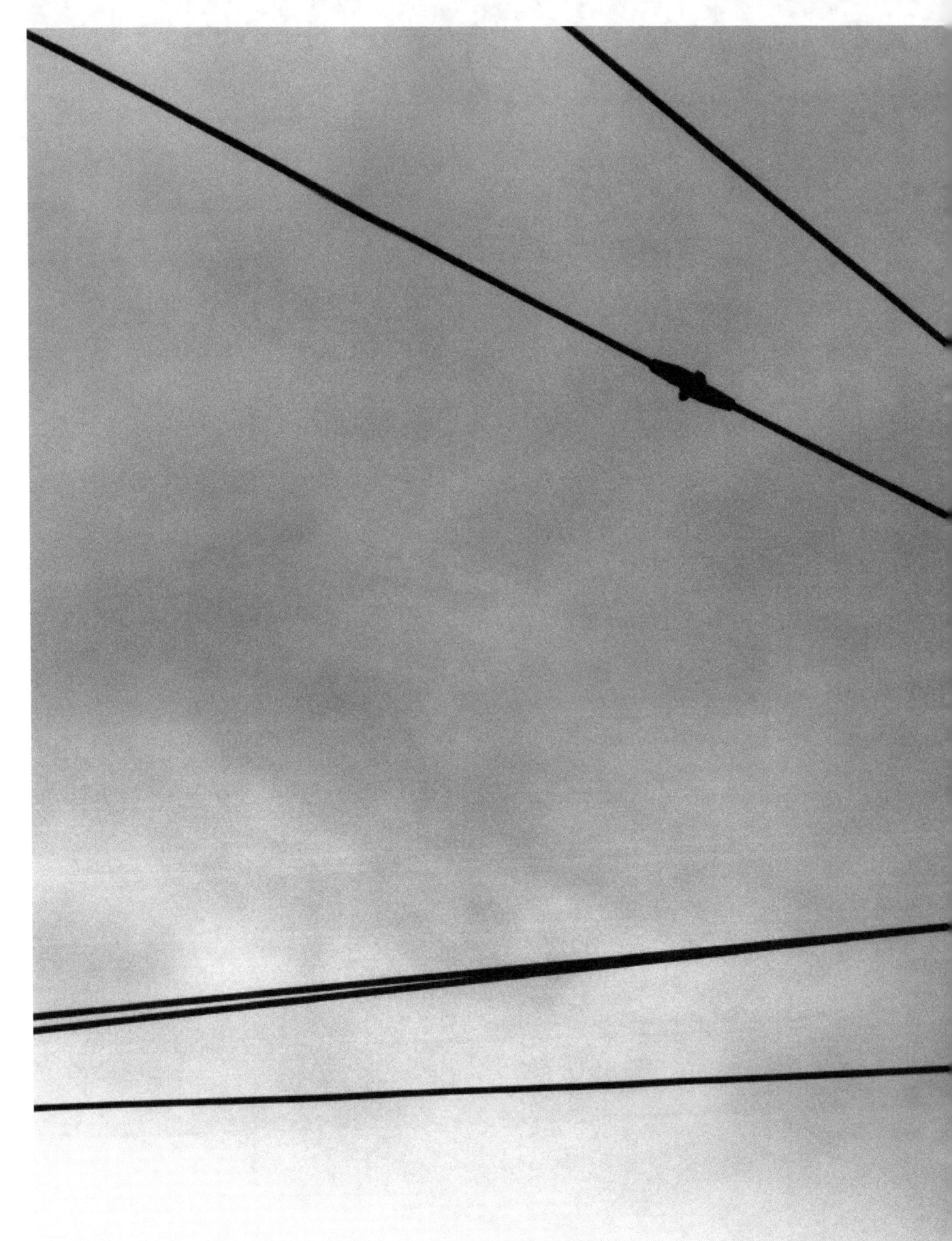

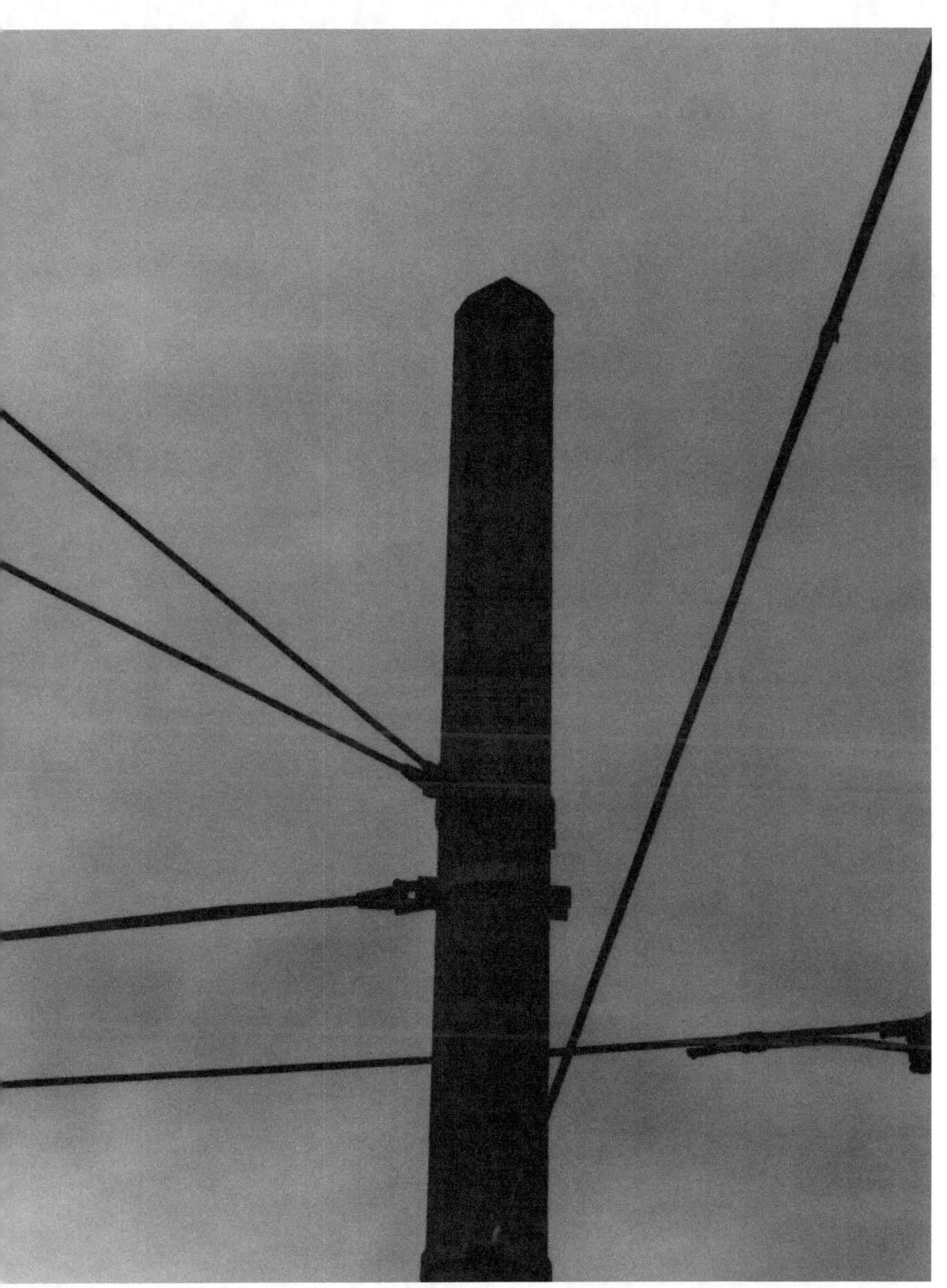

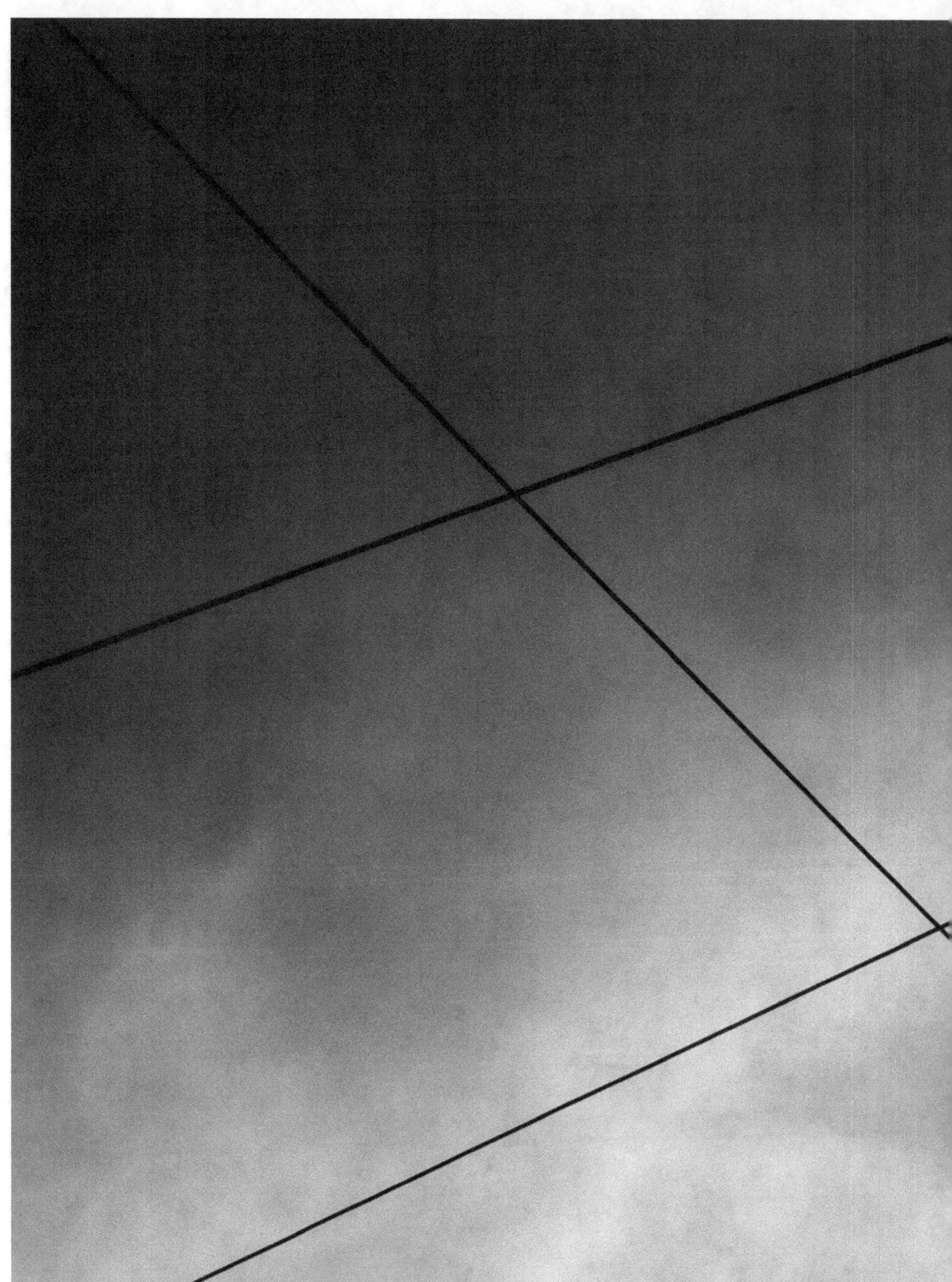

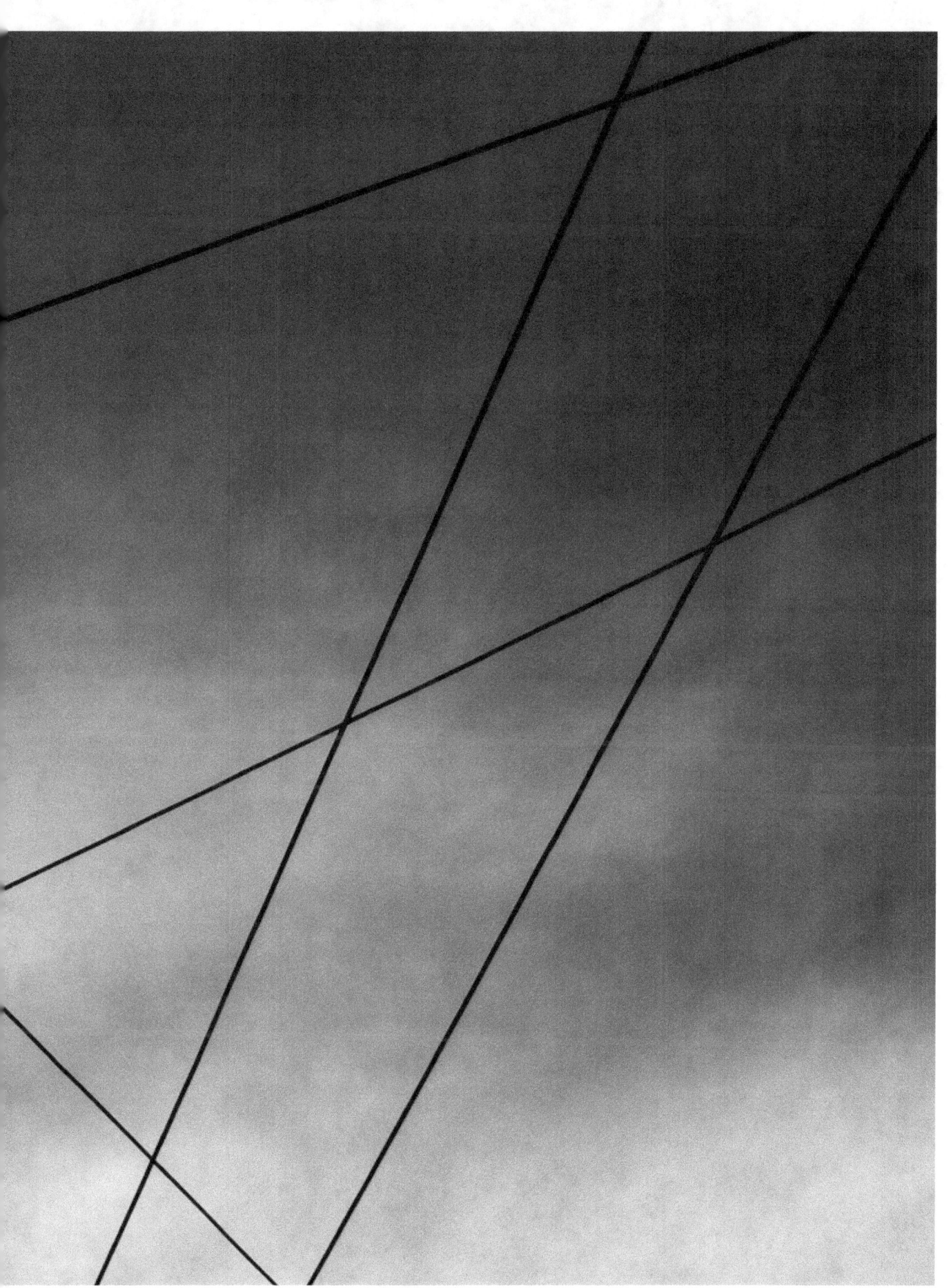

social / website

ISBN: ISBN: 9781077438927 First Printing
Published by Reader & Reader